Real Estate;
Everyone Can Afford It!

Bryan Law LLD

Disclaimer

The information contained herein has been obtained from sources that we believe are reliable but we cannot guarantee its accuracy or completeness. This book is for information only, reads should not construct this as accounting, legal or tax advice, we strongly urge that you seek professional advice prior to acting on the information contained herein.

This book is not and under no circumstances is to be construed as an intention to cause or induce the breach of, cancellation of, or assignment of any existing agreement of any person or company or to interfere in any way with the existing agreement of any person and any company.

This book is published and used on the basis and understanding that the author and publisher are to be under no responsibility or liability whatsoever in respect thereof.

Readers should consult legal counsels, accountants and/or other professionals in the related fields for specific applications to their individual situations.

© **Bryan K. Law**

All rights reserved. No part of this book may be reproduced in any form by any means, or used in any information storage and retrieval system, without the written permission of the writer.

First Edition – April 2003

Second Edition (eBook) – September 2012

Third Edition (Paperback) – January 2019

Law, Bryan K.

Real Estate; Everyone Can Afford It!

Includes index.

1. Real Estate   2. Investment

Preface

I spent one year as a high school teacher right after my university graduation. The teaching experience was excellent. I was given not only the chance to share my knowledge with my students but also the opportunity to learn how to accept different opinions. Such a great experience always reminds me of the benefits of sharing knowledge and ideas.

When I entered the profession as a real estate broker, I was given a lot of chances to gain the experiences of handling different real estate tasks. Buying and selling houses, commercial and residential leasing, investment analysis, appraising and property management are some of the fields in which I had specialized. I spent several years acquiring professional titles in different fields. During those years I had taken many real estate courses and worked with clients with different backgrounds to practice what I had learned. In order to solve my clients' problem, I created many ideas and solutions for them. Collectively, I have been able to assist all my clients in trading real estate while at the same time enriching my own real estate knowledge and experiences. Instead of teaching real estate courses and sharing my knowledge with a group of twenty people or less, I decided to write a book to share my thoughts with greater numbers.

There are so many areas to cover regarding trading in real estate. For a single chapter like Appraising Properties, it can be as long as three hundred pages, or even more. While this book will cover most fundamentals of trading in real estate, some are omitted because the main purpose is to give homebuyers and investors the important concepts in buying real estate. The ideas they should have in mind are far more important than the hands-on and how-to knowledge. To draw an analogy, you do not have to be an investment expert in stock, but you have to be smart in your own financial planning and know how to make use of services provided by investment consultants.

In trading real estate, one must have the correct concepts to be successful. For the hands-on work, one can rely on services provided by other professionals, like real estate agents, appraisers, property managers and lawyers. You should be the commander of your real estate empire, while those professionals are your generals and soldiers working for you.

Unlike articles I have submitted to professional journals where the audiences were real estate practitioners, this book was written in an easy-to-read format so that the general public can understand the concept instead of the in-depth knowledge. Thank you for reading my book.

Table of Contents

1. Benefits Of Buying Real Estate 1
   - Your Saving Bank 1
   - Personal Control 1
   - Appreciation 2
   - Leverage 3
   - Cash Income 3
   - Tax Benefits 4
   - The Land 5
   - Rent Versus Buy 6
   - The Analysis 7

2. Understanding the Real Estate Market Cycle 11
   - The Four Phases 11
   - Timing the Cycle 12
   - Using Statistics 13

3. Using Mortgages 15
   - Understanding Mortgage 15
   - How Much You Can Afford 18
   - Privileges 21
   - Restrictions and Penalty 23
   - Invest in Your Own Mortgage 23
   - Financing for Investment Properties 26
   - Source of Mortgage Funds 27
   - Owner Financing (Seller-Take-Back) 27

4. Foreclosure Properties 29
   - What Is a Foreclosure 29
   - Buying Foreclosed Properties 29
   - Inspecting Foreclosed Property 31

5. Picking the Right Property 33
   - Location 33
   - Types of Properties 33
   - Inspection 35
   - Investment Properties 35
   - Capitalization Rate 37
   - Cash on Cash 37

- The Gross Rent Problem 39
- ROI Calculations 40
- Soft Cost 42

6. Be a Landlord & a Tenant at the Same Time 44
- Purpose of Buying Real Estate 44
- Subsidize Your Rent 45
- Think Outside the Box 46
- Getting Started 47

7. How to Appraise Properties 49
- The Income Approach 49
- The Cost Approach 51
- The Direct Sales Comparison Approach 55
- Evaluate Property Before Buying 61
- Limitations 61
- Market Information 63

8. The Sources of Your Down Payment 65
- Convert Your Assets 65
- Add Up Small Savings 65
- Part-Time Job 66
- Money from the Others 67
- The 'Cheating' Clause 67
- 104 Percent Financing 70
- Buying Landlord's House 70

9. Option to Buy 72
- Option and First Right of Refusal 72
- Flipping Lands 73
- Option in a Lease 75

10. Arranging the Agreement 77
- Setting the Price 77
- The Irrevocable Time 77
- The Deposit 78
- Right to Assign 79
- The Financing Clause (Mortgage Contingency Clause) 80
- Seller-Take-Back Clause 81
- The Survey Clause 82
- The Financial Statement Clause 83
- The Inspection Clause 84
- Fixtures and Chattels 86
- Possession 87

11. Working with Real Estate Agents 89
    The Agent's Role 89
    The Duties of an Agent 93
    Choosing the Right Agent 95
    A Professional Real Estate Agent 98
    Buyer's Agency 99

12. Employing a Property Manager 102
    Property Management 102
    The Role of a Property Manager 102
    The Benefits of Employing a Property Manager 104

13. Actions to Be Taken 106
    Discussed but Not Decided! 106
    Decided but Not Acted! 106
    Acted but Not Succeeded! 107
    Act Now 108

Appendix A 110

Appendix B 112

Appendix C 114

Appendix D 116

Appendix E 119

1. Benefits Of Buying Real Estate

Through this book, I will tell you how to buy your own house by using the easiest methods and with the least risk. Before doing that, we have to see the benefits of real estate, as you may end up buying more than one property.

Most people do believe real estate is a very good investment tool, but they do not know what to choose when there are so many other investment tools on the market. Stocks, mutual funds, futures and bonds are great investment tools too, so why should they invest in real estate when they have a limited amount of capital on hand? Here are the benefits of real estate that may amaze you.

Your Saving Bank

When you buy a house with a mortgage on it you are actually saving money to a pool each month. Not mentioning other benefits below, by the time you pay off your mortgage, you will own your home. Say you buy a house and arrange a thirty-year mortgage on it. After thirty years the value of your home will be the money you have saved over that thirty years and, the important part is, the value of your home will definitely be higher than its present value after thirty years. As a matter of fact, in our history, real estate prices increase in any thirty-year interval.

Personal Control

One of the risks of buying stocks is that those listed companies are out of your control. Although there are regulations to govern all listed companies such as information that must be disclosed to investors; you are still not the one to make decisions.

Someone may argue that as a stockholder you are a part owner of the company, and are entitled to a vote. Theoretically, it is true, but practically it is not the case. Tell yourself honestly: After you bought the stock of a company, did you go to their Annual General Meeting? Did your ballot play a significant role in their decision-making? How many important meetings other than the annual general meeting would you be eligible to attend and vote?

We are not talking about a major shareholder of a listed company, but just an ordinary shareholder like you and me. Your vote may be one-millionth of the total. Of course, there are billions of dollars invested in the stock market, and I am not saying that stock is not a good investment. However, no one can deny that a real estate owner will have much more control than a minor shareholder of a large corporation.

Unlike buying stocks, buying real estate gives you full control of your holding. For example, you can make any improvement on the real property to increase its rental value as long as those improvements meet all governmental regulations. You may select your own tenants and set your own rent, as long as there is no discrimination involved and you do it according to the local regulations.

Appreciation

Almost every commodity will grow in price over years; that is why we have inflations. The prices of real estate will also go up over years, and that is the appreciation.

The price of a house may go up to $300,000, even though the house was sold for $200,000 three years ago. In some cases, people can make tens of thousands of dollars by buying and selling real estate within a short period of time; that is called flipping. My friend Bill bought a small house in Michigan for $260,000 and spent $20,000 to renovate the kitchen. He then resold it for $363,000 after several months. Although many real estate professionals discourage buying real estate to flip, it is one of the reasons real estate is so attractive.

Leverage

Other than to provide a home, a house is also an excellent investment. We have often heard that people earn big money from the stock market. Mr. Green earned $10,000 today and Mrs. Brown earned $20,000 yesterday. Other than the risk factors we have to consider, investing in stock market comparatively requires more capital to gain the same amount of profit as compared with real estate. It is because in buying real estate one can use a mortgage as leverage. Unlike speculating in the stock market by using margin accounts, using a mortgage as a leverage tool is a much safer way, and the effect is rewarding.

For example, let's say we buy a $200,000 house and we arrange a mortgage for $180,000 by paying $20,000 as the down payment. When the value of the property increases to $220,000, which is only a 10 percent increase, we have a profit of $20,000. That is a 100 percent return on investment for the $20,000 down payment we paid. Instead of using $200,000 cash to buy one house, some people will use the $200,000 as a down payment for several houses and get the benefit of leverage and average the risk. However, this is a kind of investment and carries a higher level of risk.

Cash Income

Real estate can generate cash income (the rent), just like the term deposit we have in a bank. Like the stock market, the real estate market will go up over a long run. Therefore, buy and hold is also the most common strategy in investing in real estate, and flipping is traditionally discouraged.

Since real estate generates cash income every month, some people use it to replace annuity for their retirement plan. Unlike a fixed payment paid by an annuity, the cash you are going to receive from the rental is endless and can be transferred from generation to generation. Moreover, the rent collectable may go up every year or two, making your cash flow better and better.

Tax Benefits

Under current law, you can take an income tax deduction for all property taxes you paid, and for mortgage interest on both a first and a second home (with limits of one million one hundred thousand dollars worth of borrowing). That is, real estate can lower your total taxable income.

Additionally, if the property is used as your principal residence, then its appreciation (capital gain by the increase in price) will be tax-free for the first $250,000 gain ($500,000 if you file joint returns). Based on this capital gain exemption, real estate will be, therefore, a very good 'retirement fund' if you have a large house for your family and sell the house to move down to a smaller house when you retire. Some states, such as Florida, will provide extra tax benefits for real estate buyers or owners.

First-time homebuyers may be eligible for a mortgage interest credit if your income is below the median income for the area where you live. The purpose of such credit is to help lower-income individuals to afford their own home. A tax credit is allowed each year for part of the home mortgage interest you pay.

To apply for such credit you must get a mortgage credit certificate (MCC) from your state or local government. Generally, an MCC is issued only in connection with a new mortgage for the purchase of your principal residence. You must contact the appropriate government agency about getting an MCC before you get a mortgage and before you buy your first home. However, since the laws are always changing, you should consult your accountant or lawyer for the most current tax laws in the state where you reside.

Some people will incorporate a company for the sole purpose of holding real estate. Besides the benefits of limited liabilities on the owner, it may have tax benefits when transferring company shares to the buyer instead of selling the actual property. This is used in estate planning too. Since different jurisdictions have different tax laws and real estate laws to govern such activity, you should consult your own legal counsel and accountant before acting for the same. There may be more tax benefits on real estate trust funds that you may enjoy under the Taxpayer Relief Act. Again, you should consult a tax expert for the best result in tax saving.

The Land

Unlike stocks and mutual funds, real estate will never 'vanish'. Yes, a house suffers wear and tear, needs maintenance, has a chance of burning or has to be demolished after a hundred years, but the piece of land your house is built upon will last forever.

Normally, the land value will go up with the development of the city, which is particularly true for some suburban areas. The more demand for developing the neighbourhood, the more expensive the land will be. If it is a piece of vacant land, its value may soar like a rocket if a change of zoning can be obtained in favour of the development.

Rent Versus Buy

Everyone needs a shelter. The most common question is: Should I buy my own house or keep on renting? Some people will say the answer is very obvious. As landlords earn money from the rents after paying for their mortgages and expenses, which means paying rent is definitely higher than the cost of owning a house or a condo unit. That is only one of the answers. In fact, each method of acquiring a home has its advantages and disadvantages, and the requirements differ too. In general, we can group the basic points as follows:

Advantages of renting:

1. Less capital involved. Generally, all you have to pay up-front is the two months rental deposit or even less.
2. There may be a tax deduction for rent payments.
3. Flexible for relocation. Should you wish to move to another place, instead of selling your home, you can terminate the lease at the end of the term.
4. It will not lower your borrowing power since there is no loan involved in a lease.
5. Usually, better terms can be negotiated for a rental agreement than a loan (mortgage) agreement.

Disadvantages of renting:

1. Higher operating cost. Since the landlord has to make a profit on the lease, the cost of renting is higher than the cost of owning.
2. Loss of appreciation at the end of the lease. Since a tenant does not own the property, he or she cannot enjoy the capital gain if there is any.

Advantages of Owning:

1. Greater control of the property. You can do whatever you want, within the limits of the law, on the property you own.
2. Owners have the chance to make a capital gain, which can be substantial when they sell their property. Such gain may be tax exempted, too.

Disadvantages of Owning:

1. The initial capital involved (down payment) is usually high.
2. The ability to arrange financing varies.
3. Your debt ratio goes up, which means that your borrowing power is weakened.
4. If you are living in the property, you might not be able to sell it at the best price at the best time.

These are only the basic criteria for a decision. There are, of course, more factors to be considered before you can draw a conclusion.

The Analysis

My friend Don was renting a condo unit in Ontario at $950 a month. He showed me a table he drafted that was copied from a book teaching people who were buying homes. He inserted his actual figures and asked me for advice on whether to buy his own. The table he showed me was like this:

	Monthly Mortgage Payment	Monthly Rental Payment
Year 1	$1,161	$950
Year 2	$1,161	$979
Year 3	$1,161	$1,008
Year 4	$1,161	$1,038
Year 5	$1,161	$1,069
Year 6	$1,161	$1,101
Year 7	$1,161	$1,134
Year 8	$1,161	$1,168
Year 9	$1,161	$1,203
Year 10	$1,161	$1,240
Year 11	$1,161	$1,277

He said a unit similar to the one he was renting in the same building was sold for around $100,000. For a $100,000 mortgage with a payback in ten years, he needed to pay only $1,161 a month. From the table he showed me, it was more the less the same amount of the averaged rent over ten years. The difference was that he could have his own home after ten years, mortgage free if he bought now. If he continued renting he could get nothing after ten years.

Basically, I agreed with him that buying was a better option for him, but he was too optimistic about the figures he entered (I discovered later that the book he read taught him wrong). First, he might not able to get 100 percent financing, and more importantly, he overlooked other expenses in his table.

After I had asked him for the necessary data and made some calculations, I drafted another table and showed him a more realistic comparison between owning and renting the unit as shown below.

	Mortgage Payment	Condo Fee	Property Tax (Monthly)	Total Monthly Payment	Rental Payment
Year 1	$532	$336	$130	$998	$950
Year 2	$532	$346	$130	$1,008	$979
Year 3	$532	$356	$130	$1,018	$1,008
Year 4	$532	$367	$130	$1,029	$1,038
Year 5	$532	$378	$130	$1,040	$1,069
Year 6	$532	$390	$130	$1,052	$1,101
Year 7	$532	$401	$130	$1,063	$1,134
Year 8	$532	$413	$130	$1,075	$1,168
Year 9	$532	$425	$130	$1,087	$1,203
Year 10	$532	$438	$130	$1,100	$1,240
Year 11	$532	$452	$130	$1,114	$1,277

The numbers were again based on a $100,000 purchase, but with an $80,000 mortgage (for those who are not familiar with mortgage calculations, please read Chapter 3) at 7 percent a year, amortized for thirty years, the condo fee would show a 3 percent increase, and the property tax would remain more or less the same. Rent was expected to increase 3 percent per year too.

The mortgage was based on a thirty-year amortization instead of ten years, and the total monthly payment for purchasing a unit was slightly more than the rental payment in the first three years. It started to be less than the rental payment from the fourth year onwards. In Year 9, the projected monthly payment would be lower than the projected monthly rent by more than one hundred dollars. This showed that buying a unit was a better option than renting one.

Eventually, my friend bought the same unit in a different level in the same condo building at the price of $97,000. He made a fantastic decision. The total monthly payment was actually lower than what I projected. The mortgage payment was less than five hundred dollars a month since the mortgage amount was only $77,600 and the average interest rate he paid during the ten years was only 6 percent, the condo fee was ten dollars less than my estimated one, and the property tax was increased by less than twenty dollars a month. On the other hand, most of the units in that building were rented for over $1,300, with some units (same size as his) renting for over $1,400 a month a few years later.

After 10 years, Don is paying less than $1,100 a month, which saves him more than two hundred dollars as compared to renting the same rental unit. After ten years contribution, his mortgage balance has been brought down to less than $65,000 level: Units in that building similar to his have all sold so far for more than $150,000 after 10 years. With an increase of more than $50,000 in price, plus more than $12,600 paid back to the mortgage principal, he could have made a profit of more than $60,000 if he sold his unit after 10 years.

From this example, we can see that buying your own house is a better option than renting one. The problem is that not everyone can afford to buy a house, especially those who cannot afford to pay the down payment or the house price is far above their affordability.

The purpose of this book, therefore, is to teach you how to overcome this biggest hurdle. For those who have already owned a real property, this book can show you how to expand your real estate portfolio by investing in a smarter way.

2. Understanding the Real Estate Market Cycle

Whenever there is steady economic growth and interest rates are low, real estate markets will boom for a few years and this happens from time to time. This, unfortunately, gives false hope to some people that the real estate market will go up forever. As a result, many people buy houses to flip without knowing the fundamentals of the real estate market. Most real estate speculators believed the market would continue rising when they bought properties to flip. They did not know or did not want to believe, that real estate follows a cycle.

The Four Phases

It is crucial to consider the market's phase before making real estate decisions. To know the market's phase, we have to understand that the real estate market follows a cycle. There are four phases in the cycle, namely: Recession, Recovery, Expansion and Oversupply. Knowing the nature of the four phases, we can make our decisions in trading real estate according to our objectives and the timing. That is, we make a particular strategy correspond with a particular phase.

Recession

> It usually coincides with the economic recession. Prices of properties are the lowest and it is a buyer's market. Buying real estate at this time will definitely make a profit when the market improves. Doing so is the axiom of 'buy low, sell high'. It is also the best time for first time homebuyers to buy their homes.

Recovery

> The real estate market begins to recover, prices increase from the bottom of the curve. Developers start to build as the prices may return to a profitable level to justify new construction. It is still the best time to buy, as prices are going up.

Expansion

> It is still a good time to buy, as rents will be going up as well. Everyone in the market is buying, flipping and leasing. The best time to sell real estate is at the end of the expansion phase, as prices have reached the top level.

Oversupply

> Prices and rents fall back and there is an oversupply in the market. Real estate practitioners start developing niche markets and making acquisition through the recession phase. Properties bought at this time will need a longer time to get back to the price level once the market falls.

Timing the Cycle

Investing in real estate is a long-term commitment; you should not expect it to bring you a fortune overnight, although there are many successful cases of flipping properties. Keeping in mind that a real estate cycle in North America may last for fifteen years or longer, we should expect our real estate investment to need the same period of time to perform. For example, if you buy a house at the peak time and you pay the top price for it, it really does not matter if you do not sell it until the next peak arrives. For a home, you are living in it with the same conditions no matter if its price goes up or down. For investment, the property is all right as long as it can generate positive cash flow to you. So the crucial point is not when to buy a property, it is what type of property you should buy. Buying a negative cash flow investment property will definitely cost you money, even if you buy it at the bottom price.

Although the buying time is not the most important factor, timing the cycle is rewarding and is not impossible. Since a real estate cycle usually takes ten to fifteen years, you will have enough time to 'catch up' with the market. We should not expect to buy at rock bottom and sell at the peak. All we can do is enhancing situations so that we can pay less and earn more.

After you have bought a house you can wait for a good time to sell it or to keep it for thirty years; at that time you definitely will have a gain. So one would say it is always the time to buy, but not always the time to sell.

Using Statistics

We often have to rely on statistical data when we want to study the market trend. Unfortunately, statistics are sometimes not accurate in presenting facts. For example, we are told that water at 50°C is the most comfortable temperature to our skin. If there are two buckets of water, one at 0°C and the other at 100°C; the average temperature will be 50°C. Now if you put your feet into these two buckets of water, will you feel comfortable?

Clearly not! This is just one example to show how figures can fool people. If the average price of properties in the U.S. increased by 10 percent, it does not guarantee that the price of your property in a particular neighbourhood has also grown. The reason is that 10 percent is just the average rate increased, not necessarily the 'index' of the house price in your neighbourhood.

In general, house prices reported by newspapers are in a large region, such as the whole nation, the whole state or the capital city. Furthermore, they seldom separate the prices of different properties. That is, they often include all the prices of houses, townhouses and condo units as one single type. If you want to know the price in a particular neighbourhood of a specific type of property, you should consult a real estate agent. Real estate boards provide an MLS (multiple listing services) system for their members to trade real estate; such system also provides them with the fine data of house prices, both sold prices and asking prices.

Some real estate boards provide consolidated statistical data to their members so that their real estate agents can refer to a very accurate history of the house prices in a particular district (trading zones separated by the real estate board for their own record). You may ask your real estate agent to provide you with the sale history in the district where you are looking for houses, such data is much more useful than those you find in newspapers.

3. Using Mortgages

Mortgage financing is one of the most important parts of your real estate transaction. When you sell a property you may discharge, take back or let the buyer assume a mortgage. When you buy a property you may want to arrange a new first mortgage or a second mortgage, assume the seller's mortgage or ask the seller to take back a mortgage.

Understanding Mortgage

A mortgage is simply a claim upon the real property given by the owner of the property to the lender as security for the money s/he borrowed and typically registered in the land registration office.

The lender lends the money to the owner and registers the mortgage against the property. In return, the owner makes the required periodic payments to the lender. The owner has the right to discharge the mortgage from the title once the debt is paid off or the borrowing term is matured.

Before we can calculate how much of a mortgage you can afford, we have to know some basic terms of a mortgage.

Amortization period

> When we borrow money, we have to repay it within a time frame called the amortization period. For mortgages, the amortization period can be as long as thirty years. The longer the amortization period the more interest you have to pay in total. On the other hand, the shorter the amortization period, the higher the monthly payments you have to make.

Rate

> A rate is a percentage that a lender charges as interest on the amount of money borrowed. Usually, the mortgage rate is fixed within the term, but some financial institutions provide variable rates that float with the prime rate. As the mortgage business is very competitive today, you are in a good position to negotiate a lower rate or better terms with most banks and trust companies. All the mortgage rates advertised by the financial institutions are called posted rates; they are negotiable and you may be able to get a rate 1 percent lower than the posted rate, or even better.

Term

> This is the time period that your mortgage is guaranteed by the lender. That is, the lender is committed to lending you the money for the term and cannot ask for full repayment unless you are in default of the periodic payment. When we say the term, we are also talking about the length of time that our interest rate can be fixed. It can be from six months to five years, or even longer. Rates for shorter terms are lower than those for longer terms. For example, the interest rate of a one-year closed mortgage can be 5.5 percent, while the interest rate of a five-year closed mortgage can be 7.5 percent.

Open/Closed Mortgage

> A term can be open or closed. An open mortgage allows you to pay back the loan for any amount at any time, while a closed mortgage requires you remain with that

institution for the same terms and conditions or you will be penalized. Interest rates for an open mortgage are therefore higher than for the closed mortgage for the same length of time. Lenders will seldom provide an open mortgage to run for over one year.

Prepayment

An advance payment made to the lender under a mortgage agreement can be a full or partial payment of all or part of the principal, separate and apart from regular payments.

Payment option

Many financial institutions offer payment or prepayment plans other than the standard payment terms. For example, you can pay bi-weekly instead of monthly, or increase your monthly payment to a double of the original amount. A bi-weekly payment can dramatically shorten your amortization period from thirty years to approximately twenty-three years.

Loan Ratio (Loan to Value Ratio or LTV)

This is the ratio of the principal amount of a mortgage (a loan) to the lending value (the appraised value or the purchase price, whichever is less) of the property.

Assumption

You can assume the seller's existing mortgage provided that the seller's lender agrees. When a buyer assumes the mortgage, s/he takes over the mortgage balance and becomes responsible for the payments, terms, and all monies owed. By assuming the seller's existing mortgage, you may save appraisal fees, some legal costs, and survey costs. It is particularly good for the buyer if the interest rate of the existing mortgage is lower than the current rates, although some sellers will ask for a higher price based on that. The advantage to the seller may be a savings of any payout penalty or interest differential that may apply if the seller has to discharge the mortgage before maturity.

Interest-only mortgage

On an interest-only mortgage, the borrower pays only the interest on the mortgage amount and no reduction of principal will be credited during the term. It is also known as a flat-payment mortgage.

How Much You Can Afford

As a buyer, you have many choices of arranging your payment when buying a real property. You can pay cash, arrange a new mortgage, assume the seller's mortgage or ask the seller to take back a mortgage.

If you arrange a new mortgage, you will be required to provide the lender with your proof of income and you will be qualified according to your income. A longer amortization can lower the monthly payment, and a shorter term will have a lower interest rate; both can maximize your borrowing power.

Many people will go to their financial institutions to ask for pre-approval in order to qualify themselves before buying properties. It is a good idea to do so, but you should keep in mind that such pre-approval does not guarantee that the institution will lend you the money. It is subject to such conditions as you are being employed at closing and that the house is insurable.

Besides a reasonable down payment and a good credit rating of the buyer, most lenders will consider the following ratios:

    i.   Expense-to-Income Ratio – ETI, also known as the front ratio or the housing expense ratio.

The ETI is the ratio comparing the sum of housing expenses to the borrower's gross income. The mortgage industry's conservative guideline is that housing expenses should be 28 percent or less of income.

Housing expenses (HE) include payments for principal, interest, property taxes, insurance, private mortgage insurance (if required), and condo or homeowner's fees (if required).

ETI = HE ÷ Gross Income x 100 percent.

Usually, the acceptable ETI is around 28%. In other words, your mortgage may not be approved if the housing expenses are greater than 28% of your gross income.

Some financial institutions will consider a higher ETI if the down payment is high, and most of them will use a lower ETI for a high ratio mortgage. For example, a 95% mortgage may use 25% as the standard ETI to qualify borrowers.

    ii.   Debt-to-Income Ratio – DTI (also known as the back ratio or the total debt-to-income ratio).

The DTI is the ratio of the sum of housing expenses and consumer loans to the gross income of the borrower. That is, this ratio compares the sum of debt obligations (including the prospective mortgage) to the gross income. The mortgage industry's conservative guideline is that these debt payments should be 36% or less of income. Again, different financial institutions may use different ratios for their calculations; some lenders may consider a DTI up to 50% or more.

DTI = (HE + loans) ÷ Gross Income x 100 percent

Therefore, a mortgage will be approved if both of the borrower's ETI and DTI are less than the preset percentages (say, 28% for ETI and 36% for DTI).

Example

Assume your gross family income is $50,000 per year and you are going to buy a condo unit at $190,000. Realty tax and insurance of the unit is $1,500 a year, the condo fee is $175 a month ($2,100 a year), mortgage interest rate is 7% a year, amortization period is thirty years, you have a car loan with a $5,000 balance on it and you want to apply for a 75% mortgage. The ETI and DTI guideline of your financial institution is 30% and 40%, respectively.

Price of the condo	$190,000.00
Realty taxes	$1,5000.00 per year
Condo fee	$2,100.00 per year
Other debts	$5,000.00
Family gross income	$50,000.00 per year
Mortgage rate	7% per year

Down payment required = $190,000 x (1-75 percent)
 = $190,000 x 25 percent
 = $47,500.00

Mortgage amount = $190,000 x 75 percent
 = $142,500.00

The monthly mortgage payment, at an interest rate of 7 percent a year, is $948.06. The annual payment is $11,376.72.

ETI = HE ÷ Gross Income x 100 percent
 = ($11,376.72 + $1,500.00 + $2,100.00) ÷ $50,000.00 x 100 %
 = $14,976.72 ÷ $50,000.00 x 100%
 = 29.95%

DTI = (HE + loans) ÷ Gross Income x 100 percent
 = ($11,376.72 + $1,500 + $2,100 + $5,000) ÷ $50,000 x 100%
 = $19,780.24 ÷ $50,000.00 x 100%
 = 39.95%

Since the ETI is less than 30% and DTI is less than 40%, your mortgage is preliminarily approved!

Privileges

Some benefits of a mortgage are not rights under the mortgage document, but just privileges. You have to have the privileges spelt out in your mortgage document in order to enjoy them. The most common privileges are:

Prepayment Privilege

Some lenders will allow you to repay part of the

mortgage amount before the maturity of the term; it is called the prepayment privilege. Usually, they will allow you to pay back 10% to 20% of the original mortgage amount each year. This is useful when the mortgage rate is high at the time you sign your mortgage document. You may wish to pay it back by applying for another loan once the interest rate drops to a lower level.

Renewal Privilege

Do not assume your mortgage will automatically be granted for renewal upon maturity of the term, although it is always the case for most financial institutions. Some mortgage documents have a built-in renewal privilege, but some do not, especially for the seller-take-back mortgage. If the mortgage document does not specifically spell out the opportunity to renew, then this privilege does not exist. You should always ask for this privilege when arranging a mortgage.

Transfer Privilege

This is also known as assumption privilege. This provides for someone, usually the buyer, to assume the existing mortgage with the same terms and conditions. Although the mortgage is assumed by another person, the lenders usually include a provision in the mortgage document that they can hold the original borrower liable if the mortgage is in default by the one who assumed it. You should be cautious when you are the seller and want someone to assume your mortgage.

Portable Privilege

When the owner moves to another house, s/he may need to discharge her/his existing mortgage and arrange a new one for her/his new home. In order to avoid the penalty for early discharge of the existing mortgage, a portable privilege should be asked for. When you sell your home and buy another one, portability enables you to transfer your mortgage from your existing house to your new one without paying any penalty. In some cases you will have to discharge the mortgage and pay the penalty first, The lender will reimburse you once the new mortgage signed with them goes into effect.

Restrictions and Penalty

Although we may have the transfer privilege in our mortgage document, it does not mean that the assumption will be automatically approved. The transfer privilege has some preset conditions to meet. For example, the buyer, the one who is going to assume the mortgage, must have a good credit history and her/his income must be high enough to afford the payments.

If you discharge a closed mortgage before the maturity date, you will be penalized a sum of money by the lender. Most financial institutions charge three months interest as penalty for early discharge or six months interest differential, whichever is higher. It can cost you thousands of dollars depending on the terms and conditions. Some institutions may charge six months interest or even more. You must learn from your lender the penalty for discharging a mortgage before you commit with them.

Invest in Your Own Mortgage

Unless there is a benefit in paying the interest (such as using the mortgage as leverage and the interest paid is lower than the rate of return), you should avoid paying too much interest on the mortgage. Even though the interest paid on a mortgage is tax deductible, saving $1 in interest is better than getting $.50 (or less) tax refund from the government.

When you have one thousand dollars in your pocket and want to invest, it seems that there are not many investment tools you can choose. Investing in your own mortgage is a very rewarding investment option and is 100 percent safe. For example, you have a mortgage in the amount of $150,000 at an interest rate of 7% per year, amortized for thirty years. Your monthly payment will be $ 997.95 as shown on Payment Schedule A.

Payment Schedule A (normal payment, $997.95 per month)

Month	Principal Paid	Interest Paid	Balance
11	$130.32	$867.64	$148,607.36
12	$131.08	$866.88	$148,476.28
13	$131.84	$866.11	$148,344.44
14	$132.61	$865.34	$148,211.83
15	$133.38	$864.57	$148,078.45
16	$134.16	$863.79	$147,944.28
17	$134.95	$863.01	$147,809.34
18	$135.73	$862.22	$147,673.61
19	$136.52	$861.43	$147,537.08
20	**$137.32**	**$860.63**	**$147,399.76**
21	$138.12	$859.83	$147,261.64
22	$138.93	$859.03	$147,122.71

If you pay back one thousand dollars to the mortgage (the prepayment) on the thirteenth month, then the original payment schedule will change to Payment Schedule B. You can see that when you pay back $1,000 in the thirteenth month, the remaining balance jumps to the amount that is less than the balance in the twentieth month in Payment Schedule A. That is, the payment schedule is shortened by more than seven months, which is equal to a saving of more than $7,000. This is because when you pay the fourteenth payment in Payment Schedule B, you are actually paying more or less the twenty-first payment in Payment Schedule A (since the balance of the 13th payment after $1,000 in Schedule B is more or less the balance of the 20th payment in Schedule A). That is to say, you have saved more than seven monthly payments. In other words, you have a return on investment more than 700 percent, instantly!

Payment Schedule B (paid $1,000 more in the 13th month)

Month	Principal Paid	Interest Paid	Balance
11	$130.32	$867.64	$148,607.36
12	$131.08	$866.88	$148,476.28
13	**$1,131.84**	**$8606.11**	**$147,344.44**
...			
...			
20	**$137.32**	**$860.63**	**$147,399.76**
21	$138.12	$859.83	$147,261.64
22	$138.93	$859.03	$147,122.71
...			
...			

Why is there a more than 700 percent return on the $1,000 invested in (payback to) the mortgage? Simply speaking, it is because the one thousand dollars is repaid in the second year to lower the debt. In other words, the balance of the mortgage is reduced by $1,000 for the remaining of the amortization period. By compounding the $1,000 on 7 percent annually for nearly thirty years, it will accumulate an astonishing interest. That is, the return is actually the saving in total interest payable for the $1,000 compounded over twenty-nine years. In today's low deposit interest rate, putting your money back to your mortgage is both a safe and high return 'investment'.

Financing for Investment Properties

The loan ratio for commercial mortgages is usually lower than for residential mortgages due to the higher risk level. You may be qualified for arranging a 100 percent mortgage on a house, but the highest loan ratio in commercial real estate (first mortgage) hardly exceeds 70 percent. If you are buying a condo unit for investment purpose (to rent it out), it may be under the commercial category too, depending on the financial institution you choose.

Most commercial lenders will require a report on estimated income/operating expenses and the borrower's information. The report on estimated income/operating expenses contains full details of estimated gross operating income, projected vacancy rates, general expenses (excluding debt service), and net operating income. The borrower's information should include a credit report on the borrower and the background of the company/directors if it is under a company's name.

If it concerns a vacant land, then a construction and site analysis may also be needed. A construction and site analysis is documentation regarding the property, architectural drawings, detailed construction plans, utilities, landscaping, parking, buffer zones, adjacent zoning, and zoning amendments required. It can be a brief letter in point form or a fully detailed report.

For industrial properties, a soil test is a must and a phase one environmental report is often requested too. Some financial institutions will request a soil test for all types of investment properties, including commercial plazas, stores, plus apartments and rental apartments. The cost for a soil test can be thousands of dollars or more.

It is very common for the seller to take back a mortgage (first or second) in selling commercial properties. Again, you should ask for the renewal privilege in the offer. Since a commercial mortgage is comparatively more difficult to arrange than a residential one, without a renewal privilege it may ruin your whole investment plan.

Source of Mortgage Funds

While banks and trust companies are the most common places to shop for mortgages, small financial institutions and private lenders are other good sources of loans. Private lenders can be your parents, relatives and friends; a stranger investor found in the newspapers or the 'hidden' investor introduced by your mortgage broker.

The biggest difficulty for most people in shopping for their own mortgages is that they do not know how to ask the right questions and hence do not know how to choose the best terms to fit their requirements. Instead of shopping among lenders yourself, you can rely on a mortgage broker.

Mortgage brokers have access to many types of loan programs, Some of them may submit your application to many lenders, and therefore can shop around for the best and most competitive mortgage rates and terms available, tailored to meet your particular needs. Most mortgage brokers do not charge a fee, but some charge a processing fee, or so-called origination fee. It can be waived in some cases.

Owner Financing (Seller-Take-Back)

You may ask the seller to take back a mortgage if you do not have enough amount of down payment or the bank does not lend you enough money to buy what you want. This is often arranged as a second mortgage or even a third mortgage. The major difference between a first mortgage and a second mortgage is that the first mortgage has a higher priority for redeeming the property if the borrower is in default. In other words, a second mortgage has a higher risk than a first mortgage and the third mortgage has a higher risk than a second mortgage, and so on. Because of that, the interest rate charged for a second mortgage is usually higher than for the first mortgage; say by one or two percent.

In response to a seller-take-back mortgage request, the seller will often insert a condition in the offer requiring a satisfactory check of the buyer's credit in order to protect herself/himself. It will be of mutual benefit for both seller and buyer when the buyer assumes the seller's mortgage if the interest rate of that mortgage is lower than the market rate. The buyer can then enjoy a lower interest rate and the seller will not be penalized by the bank. However, such an assumption has to be approved by the lender who granted the original mortgage.

Once again, you are reminded to have the renewal and prepayment privileges included in your mortgage document if you want the seller to take back a mortgage.

4. Foreclosure Properties

What Is a Foreclosure

Foreclosure is a procedure in which a property pledged as security for a debt is sold to pay the debt in event of default in payments or terms. When the mortgage payment is in default, the creditors (usually banks) may exercise their right to force the sale of the property. The property owner is still liable for the shortage if there are not sufficient funds to pay back the creditor, including all expenses incurred. On the other hand, the creditor will pay back any surplus to the owner after deducting all disbursements.

Although some states have anti-deficiency laws which protect homeowners from being held responsible for any deficiency in foreclosure if there is any deficit between the sale proceeds and the outstanding loan balance, it does not affect the buyer at all. A buyer of a foreclosed property will still get a clean title without any problem in those states.

Buying Foreclosed Properties

Many people think foreclosure properties are a bargain to buy. This is not necessarily correct. We must understand that although the creditor has the right to force the sale of property under foreclosure, the creditor also has the responsibility to sell the property at a reasonable price (not to forget that any surplus has to be paid back to the property owner). There are cases in which owners sued their creditors for selling their foreclosed properties for too low prices. As a result, creditors will not list a house for sale at a lower price, if only to protect them from being sued. Consequently, the asking price of a foreclosure property will not be lower than a normal sale.

In addition, some owners could not accept the fact that their houses were being sold under foreclosure and knew perfectly well that the final sale price was insufficient to cover the outstanding loan balance. As a result, they could not control their temper and intentionally damaged the house. Broken walls, messy floors, broken doors and windows were the most common problems found in such properties. Consequently, the sale prices of these properties were lower than the market prices. That was because the conditions of the houses were far below average, not because of foreclosure. Moreover, since the buyer must spend some money to restore the property to the original condition, the final cost of the property would then be the same as an ordinary sale or even at a higher price.

Another factor that affects the sale of a foreclosed property is that many people believe foreclosure properties are a bargain and will compete with each other and hence jack up the price. Keep in mind that a foreclosure is a 'force' to sell the property, not a sale under its market value.

If you want to buy a foreclosure property at a lower price, you should NOT act fast. Hurrying to compete with other buyers will raise the price to a higher level, and submitting your offer too soon will make creditors feel that the price has been set at a very attractive level and they will be reluctant to lower it. The best way is to WAIT for two months or so. The reason is that if the house cannot be sold after two months, the creditor will consider lowering its price. Waiting for a period of time before lowering the price is the best way for the creditor to tell the property owner: Time has already proved that the asking price was not set well to attract buyers, and lowering the price is the only solution.

This approach, however, has a weak point, which is the property may have been sold before you can submit an offer to the creditor. However, you should have no regrets if the foreclosure property is sold at a fair market price or even at a higher price.

In some jurisdictions, property owners will be allowed the last chance to redeem their foreclosed property before closing even if the property has been sold to a third party (with a provision in the agreement). To eliminate this possibility, a buyer of a foreclosure property will always set the closing date very soon.

Inspecting Foreclosed Property

Generally speaking, creditors of foreclosure properties will not allow an inspection clause in the offer, but it does not mean that buyers cannot inspect a foreclosed property. There are two possible ways to inspect a foreclosed property. First, the sellers of foreclosure properties may not be large corporations such as banks and trust companies. They may be individual investors, and therefore are more flexible to deal with and may accept an inspection clause in the offer. Secondly, no matter whether the seller is a person or a bank; the buyer may also request an inspection before submitting an offer. Such a request will usually be entertained.

Having an inspection clause in the offer is better because you will have already 'secured' the purchase before spending money for the inspection. You do not have to worry about another buyer competing with you once the inspection is passed. Therefore, the first option gives you better protection.

If you are going to do the inspection first before submitting an offer, you should ask the seller's agent to see if there is already an offer under negotiation or registered on it. If not, you should arrange the inspection as soon as possible and submit your offer right after the inspection has been made to avoid competition.

Such a method includes a little bit of risk, as a competing buyer may appear at any time before your offer is accepted by the seller. You might lose the deal, and thus the money spent for inspection would be wasted. Even if there is no other buyer to compete with you; the final price offered by the seller (the creditor) may not be acceptable to you. That means you would lose the inspection fee. But for peace of mind, some buyers will still take this approach

5. Picking the Right Property

Location

All of us know the most important factor affecting the price of a real property is its location. Just imagine, a unit in a high-rise condo building in Buffalo sold for $100,000; it could have sold for over one million dollars if the building were located in downtown Tokyo.

Selecting a good location is important for both residential and commercial properties. Commercial properties need traffics, while residential properties need privacy. As a result, corner lots in the downtown core are good for commercial plazas but may not suitable for houses.

Types of Properties

Other than high-rise buildings, most of the real properties in North America built after World War II are constructed of wood. When we refer to an all brick house, we probably mean the all-brick-veneer house. Most of our houses are built with wood and then covered by brick, stone, aluminum, stucco or pressure-treated wood, which provides a weathertight skin and protection against intruders, both animal and human. The interior is still, in most cases, of wood construction. Therefore, you must make sure that the house you are going to buy is well maintained and that there is no latent problem in the wood.

Ownerships of real properties can be freehold, condominium (condo), cooperative (coop) and timesharing, or a mix of them. All kinds of ownership can be found in any type of structure. That is, a condo can be a high-rise building, a townhouse complex, a commercial plaza or houses. On the other hand, there are freehold townhouses and freehold high-rise buildings (all the units in a rental apartment belong to the same owner).

Generally speaking, we can classify real properties (by structure) as detached houses, semi-detached houses, townhouses (or row houses), low-rise and high-rise buildings. Freehold houses have the highest value among all the others as it has the biggest flexibility in re-development. Theoretically, you may demolish your house and rebuild a new one whenever you like as long as the new house meets all the building requirements of your local authorities.

When you buy freehold property do not forget to ask for the survey. Sometimes the property may have an encroachment (an unauthorized intrusion onto the lands of your neighbour) and a survey can tell you if there is a problem. For those who want to buy a condo unit or other co-sharing properties, do not forget to ask for the financial statement of the corporation. A suitable clause should be included in your offer (see Chapter 10).

My friend Joe bought a bungalow in the Niagara area in 1977. A few days before closing, he received a call from his lawyer saying that the bank refused to lend him the money as they found there was an encroachment in the property. Joe phoned his bank immediately and was told that part of the detached garage of the property was built on the property beside it. Joe was so surprised that this encroachment was not shown on the survey. Eventually, Joe had to pay a thousand dollars more to the seller as compensation for the delay in closing as he had to find another financial institution that would lend him the closing fund. When he told me this story in 1997, he still did not know what went wrong and how to prevent it from happening again. I explained to him that the survey he received was out of date. He should have asked for an up-to-date survey for his property instead of an existing one in order to ensure that there was no encroachment. An up-to-date survey can show the most potential problems associated with the land.

Inspection

We can tell if people are really sick when we see them in the hospital. However, even a doctor may not be able to tell whether a person is sick without doing a blood test or scanning if the illness is a hidden one. The same applies to real estate. Most people can tell if a house is well maintained or not, but they do not know whether the house has any hidden deficiency that will cause problems.

I strongly encourage you to employ a professional home inspector if peace of mind is important to you. Having an inspection done by a professional home inspector can give not only peace of mind but also precious advice to keep your home in good shape.

Investment Properties

Other than lands, residential and commercial properties are the two main types of investment property. These two kinds of investment have their own pros and cons.

Since states and cities have their own legal procedures and/or laws to deal with the residential tenancy, landlords have many restrictions with respect to their rights. On the other hand, the capital required to invest in residential properties is relatively less than that for commercial properties and the vacancy rate is lower than that in commercial because everyone requires a roof. However, the bad debt ratio can be higher than in commercial.

In most jurisdictions, there is no specific law governing the leasing of commercial properties. That means an owner of commercial property can evict tenants for not paying rent much more easily than a residential property owner. Terms and conditions are set out in the lease and the landlord will have the upper hand most of the time. However, the vacancy rate is higher than in residential units as not everybody needs to carry business, and not every business is successful. This is particularly true during a recession.

The differences between residential and commercial investment properties are summarized as follows:

	Residential	Commercial
Examples	Condo units Condo town houses Multiple complex	Industrial units Strip plaza Store/Apartment
Typical Rate of Return	2 percent to 8 percent	5 percent to 14 percent
Typical Capital Investment	$50,000 and up	$250,000 and up
Typical Term of Lease	1−2 years	3−10 years
Type of rent	Most are gross rent (Rent includes all expenses and tax)	Most are net rent (All expenses and tax are extra)
Appraised Value	Determined by the neighborhood of the property	Determined by the income generated by the property

Some people like to invest in a store plus apartment in a well-developed area like a downtown core. The reason is this type of property averages out the advantages and disadvantages between residential and commercial properties. The potential of re-development is also a factor to consider.

A rule of thumb is: Never buy any real estate that generates negative cash flow (see how to calculate cash flow in the later section) unless you are a professional and know how to flip or redevelop the property.

Capitalization Rate

There are many ways to calculate the rate of return on investment. The two most common and easiest methods in real estate are the capitalization rate and the cash on cash.

Capitalization rate (cap rate) is the ratio between the annual net operating income and sale price. Net operating income is the total rent collectible after all expenses and allowance. A worksheet to help you to calculate the net operating income is printed in Appendix A.

The higher the capitalization rate, the shorter the time needed to recover the capital (the purchase price). Usually, investors will look for properties with a cap rate of 8 percent or higher, depending on the location of the properties.

Capitalization rate = Annual net operating income ÷ Sale price of the property

Cash on Cash

Many investors have only one equation in their mind when they decide to buy real estate as an investment. The projected rent has to be high enough to pay the mortgage payments, realty taxes and maintenance fees. They believe their investments are then guaranteed, since the rents collectible are high enough to pay all those expenses, and will make reasonable profits over years.

Using this strategy to invest in real estate is like gambling. There are usually some expenses that those investors have forgotten to consider, such as agent's commission, maintenance cost, vacancy cost and bad debt. All of these 'forgotten' expenses may result in the income statement being negative. When the real estate market is hot, they can sell the property and make a profit. If the market is down, however, they will have to pay for the shortage every year or sell it at a loss.

The most common problem encountered in real estate investments is that the property could not generate positive cash flow to the owner. The proper investment strategy is to make sure of a positive rate of return (usually higher than the interest rate of a term deposit) from the property so that the investor need not sell her/his properties under pressure. The investors then will consider selling their properties only when the real estate market goes up or the capital allowance has been used up for sheltering taxes. You have to know how to calculate the cash flow of an investment property and to project it for a couple of years before deciding to buy it. By doing a projection on cash flow, you will know if you need extra money to 'feed' your property when it is 'hungry'. It is often called a cash flow analysis. A sample worksheet to help you to do a cash flow analysis on a property is printed in Appendix B.

It is logical to ask this question: I have paid this amount of money (cash); how much cash income can this property produce for me? In order to compare the cash output from different properties, the rate cash on cash is used. Actually, cash on cash is one of the yields of an investment. It is the ratio of the cash flow generated by the property to the money you have initially invested in that property. That is:

Cash on cash = Cash flow before taxes ÷ initial money invested

Use the worksheet in Appendix A to calculate the cash flow before taxes. Once you know the cash flow before taxes generated by the property, you can find the cash on cash of it.

The Gross Rent Problem

One day an excited client showed me an advertisement in a local newspaper. It was a plaza for sale and she believed it would be a very good investment. It was a three-unit free-standing commercial plaza on a corner. The owner claimed the rate of return was 12 percent and asked for $1.1 million. It was located in the downtown core and had ample parking spaces.

It was too good to be true, as the market was looking for only 8 percent rate of return at that time, so I called the owner to ask for details. After a detailed analysis, I found that the actual rate of return of that plaza was less than 7 percent, as the method that the seller used was incorrect (maybe he intentionally did it wrong). Moreover, all leases were calculated in gross rent and on a monthly basis, which was not good for commercial properties. I, therefore, advised my client not to buy it.

The plaza was sold after one month and I indirectly knew the new owner, as he was a friend of my cousin. My cousin told me soon after the closing date that one of the three tenants moved out and another tenant closed his business at the same time. This made the rate of return drop to less than 3 percent. Just when the new owner rented out the two units, he received a notice from the city saying that there would be a special assessment on his property, and the levy was $6,000. Since all the leases he signed were gross rent lease, that meant he had to pay the $6,000 himself.

Most commercial leases are based on net rent; therefore, realty taxes and maintenance fees are extra fees to be paid by the tenants. If the leases signed by the owner of the abovementioned plaza were all net-rented, he could have transferred the responsibility of paying the levy to his tenants so that he would not have to pay that $6,000.

ROI Calculations

The item most people omit in calculating return on investment (ROI) is the vacancy and bad debt allowance. Omitting them would show a higher rate of return. Following are two simple examples to show the correct way to find the rate of return for residential and commercial properties.

Example 1: Investment in Residential Property (Condo Unit)

You are buying a condo unit at $110,000. The condo fee is $350 a month, realty tax is $2,000 a year and the projected rent is $1,200 a month. You will pay $55,000, as the down payment; the current mortgage rate is 7.5 percent a year and with thirty years amortization. The capitalization rate and cash-on-cash are calculated below:

	Monthly	Yearly
Rent	$ 1,200	$14,400
Condo fee	$ 350 (-)	$ 4,200 (-)
Realty taxes		$ 2,000 (-)
Vacancy and bad debt allowance* (10 percent)		$ 1,440 (-)
Non-recoverable expenses**		$ 1,000 (-)

40

Net income before debt		$ 5,760

Price for the unit	=	$110,000
Capitalization Rate	=	$ 5,760 ÷ $110,000 x 100%
	=	5.24%

Down payment (50 percent)	$55,000
Mortgage payment at 7.5%, amort. 30 years	$ 4,615 a year

Net operating income after debt	=	$ 5,760 - $ 4,615
	=	$ 1,145

Cash on Cash	=	$ 1,145 ÷ $55,000 x 100%
	=	2.08%

* The vacancy and bad debt allowance is based on the history of the property and the present economic situation.

** Non-recoverable expenses include all expenses that were not covered in the maintenance fee; such as the fee for a property manager. It does not exist in a lease drafted in a way that the maintenance fee covers all expenses, which the landlord must pay out of her/his pocket.

Example 2: Investment in Commercial Property (Strip Plaza)

You bought a strip plaza for $750,000 with 30 percent down payment. The mortgage rate was 7.5 percent a year, amortized over thirty years. The rental income was $75,788 a year. The cap rate and cash on cash are calculated below (all figures are per year):

	Yearly
Rent	$75,788
Maintenance fee	Recoverable
Realty taxes	Recoverable

Vacancy and bad debt allowance* (4 percent)		$3,032 (-)
Non-recoverable expenses**		$8,200 (-)
Net operating income before debt		$64,556

Price for the plaza = $750,000

Capitalization Rate = $64,556 ÷ $750,000 x 100%
 = 8.61%

Down payment paid (30%) = $750,000 x 30%
 = $225,000

Mortgage payment = $44,051
(7.5%, 30 years amortization)

Net income after debt = $64,556 − $44,051
 = $20,505

Cash on Cash = $20,505 ÷ $225,000 x 100%
 = 9.11%

* The vacancy and bad debt allowance is based on the history of the property and the present economic situation.

** Non-recoverable expenses include all expenses that were not covered in the maintenance fee; such as the fee for a property manager. It does not exist in a lease drafted in a way that the maintenance fee covers all expenses, which the landlord must pay out of her/his pocket.

Soft Cost

Soft cost is the fee you must pay other than the costs (purchase price) of building and land. Soft costs are normally associated with service fees, including legal fee, mortgage broker's fee, real estate agent's commission and realty taxes. It is important to know the soft cost before you decide to buy or sell a property.

For example, you bought a house for $200,000 two years ago. Now the price of your house has increased to $218,000. It seems that you will get $8,000 in profit from the sale of your house if the total commission for selling your house is $10,000. However, you may end up with a loss since you did not include the soft cost paid when you bought the house.

When you calculate sale proceeds, you must know the soft cost of your purchase. A sample worksheet to calculate the sales proceeds is included in Appendix C for your reference.

Many first time investors overlook soft cost when they calculate their budget and return on investment. Consequently, they buy properties below average performances or fall into a tight cash flow situation.

6. Be a Landlord & a Tenant at the Same Time

Many people live in their own houses. Some live in their own mansions and are landlords with quite a few rental properties. Many people still rent houses, as they think they can not afford to buy one. A small portion of people live in rental properties, and on the other hand, own their own rental properties as an investment. Most of those did that because they had to move to another neighbourhood but could not afford to buy a house there or did not want to sell their existing home at a loss. Instead of selling their existing home they simply rented it out, and rent another one in the new neighbourhood where they moved. They are, therefore, a landlord and a tenant at the same time. Just a few of them did that in purpose as an investment. Being a landlord and a tenant at the same time is, in fact, a good solution for those who cannot afford to buy their own home to live in.

Purpose of Buying Real Estate

We have seen the benefits of investing in real estate in chapter one, so we should know real estate is indeed a good investment. In fact, the purpose of buying real estate is more than to have a home to live in; it is also an investment in your future. In other words, real estate should either increase your cash flow (when it is an investment property) or lower your expense (when it is your principal residence). In both cases, it has the ability to appreciate.

If you cannot afford to buy the type of house you are now renting, try to buy a smaller house or a house in a less expensive neighbourhood. By doing so, you are on board to success in real estate investment. It is the most crucial move.

Say you have five members in your family and you are renting a house. The smallest house that can accommodate your needs is a three-bedroom. Unfortunately, the lowest price of a three-bedroom house in your neighbourhood is $200,000, while you can afford only a $100,000 mortgage. You have been saving for years and all you have is $5,000 in the bank It seems impossible for you to buy your own house. You wait and wait, working hard, hoping that your savings will grow enough to pay the down payment or you will get a promotion so that your job can qualify for a higher mortgage. At that time you can fulfill your dream—to have your own house. By the time you have saved $50,000 in your bank account and you are qualified for a $150,000 mortgage, you go out to shop for a house. You believe you can finally afford your own house, but you find that the price of such a house has been increased from $200,000 to $250,000 or even more.

If you want to race the house price by your wage, you will probably lose. If the price of your 'dream home' is far above your budget, you might not be able to buy it after years of hard working and saving. From the example above, the solution is to buy a property within the $110,000 price, the one you can afford, and then wait for the chance to move up. It does not matter if it is a two-bedroom bungalow or even a bachelor suite in a condo building. Buy the property and rent it out. You then are on the way to be a successful landlord who is wealthy and successful in real estate investment.

Subsidize Your Rent

In the above example, it is a good idea to buy a $100,000 house and rent it out while you are still renting a house that costs $200,000 to buy. The two main benefits of doing that are:

1. You are finally a property owner. A real estate is now a reachable tool for you to increase your wealth.

2. The rent you receive from your house can subsidize the rent you are paying.

If you live in a city like New York, Boston, Los Angeles or Philadelphia, where all house prices are extremely high and you cannot even afford buying the smallest house there, you may still have an alternative.

Every major city is surrounded by smaller cities and suburban neighbourhoods. The rates of return on investment in those surrounding areas are usually higher than in the major cities. The rent collected from a house in a remote area may subsidize your rental and in some cases, may even provide a surplus.

My friend Paul worked in New York, the most expensive city to live in. He thought he could never buy his own house, as the houses in New York were far above his affordability. Soon after he heard this idea from me, he bought a house in Rochester and rented it out. That turned out to be a very successful investment and subsidized his rental for several years. The five-hour drive from New York to Rochester was nothing to him, as he needed to go there only twice or three times a year. The earning power was the drive, especially when it was a chance to fulfill his dream to be a landlord.

He is now working in Toronto and still keeps the house in Rochester. The 'subsidy' becomes a surplus, as the rent he pays for a one-bedroom unit in Toronto is lower than the rental he earns from that house in Rochester. Moreover, the driving time is shortened. It takes him only two hours to travel from Toronto to Rochester, which makes property management easier.

Think Outside the Box

Even if all house prices in your city and surrounding areas are far beyond your affordability, there is still a solution.

When you relocate from a smaller city to a large city that is more expensive to live in, say, from Florence, South Carolina, to San Diego, California, you may not wish to sell your existing property. Renting out your existing home and using it as your income-generating machine is an alternative. If it is hard to buy a house that can accommodate your needs in the city that you are relocating to, why not keep your existing house in your mother town and use it to produce income for you? You may even wish to buy a house in your mother town before you relocate to another state so that you can rent it out before you depart.

Overseas investors come to the U.S. to buy real estate every year, some from nearby Canada and South American countries, but some from the Far East, like Japan and Hong Kong. People from the Far East can fly over eighteen hours to buy properties here to invest, so why can't you make a one day trip to buy a house in other cities or areas near where you live. Or why not simply keep your existing house or buy another one in your mother town when you are required to relocate?

I am not suggesting you leave your house to your tenant without taking care of it. Absentee landlords have been the cause of many blighted and run-down neighbourhoods. You must have someone, a friend or a relative, who is competent in dealing with rental matters to take care of your property. Otherwise, you should employ a property manager to look after it. We will discuss the benefits of employing a property manager in Chapter 12.

Getting Started

Write down names of cities near the one where you reside and the cities where you have relatives and friends who can take care of a rental unit for you. Search for houses on the Internet to learn house prices there. Search for houses for rent to get an idea about the rental market in those cities. Compare house prices among these cities for those you can afford and manage easily. Make a trip to those selected areas and physically inspect the houses with a local real estate agent. For those cities too far away to visit by driving, you may spend your vacation there and find out more.

The first move is always the most difficult. Do not make more excuses. If you want to have your own house in the near future, make the first move now.

7. How to Appraise Properties

When people want to sell their home, they will always ask real estate agents to provide them with a 'market value evaluation'. A market value evaluation is, in fact, an appraisal, although it is simple and not detailed, compared to a formal appraisal. The purpose is to estimate the market value of the subject property so that the seller can know the expected sale price and set the right asking price in order to sell it within a reasonable time.

Market value has been defined as the "highest price estimated in terms of money which a property would bring if exposed for sale on the open market by a willing seller, allowing a reasonable time to find a willing buyer, neither buyer nor seller acting under compulsion, both having full knowledge of the uses and purposes to which the property is adapted, and for which it is being used".

A recent definition that has evolved and is gaining popularity: "the most probable price that the property would bring if sold in the open market, at terms of sale currently predominant for properties of this type".

Three methods of approach are normally utilized in the appraisal process and involve a systematic analysis of factors that affect the value of the real estate. They are the Income Approach, Cost Approach and Direct Sales Comparison Approach. One or a combination of all three of the methods may be selected in the appraisal, decided by the appropriateness in the application to an individual property.

The Income Approach

One method of estimating value is to convert net income of a real property into capital value and evaluate the present worth of the future benefits accrued through the ownership of an income producing property.

This approach reflects an investor's attitude to a property's net income since it is directly related to the rate of return on her/his capital investment and of her/his depreciating asset.

The steps of the Income Approach are:

i) Estimate the annual gross income.
ii) Estimate and deduct from the gross income the income loss through vacancy and bad debt to arrive at effective gross income.
iii) Estimate and deduct from the effective gross income all annual operating expense to arrive at the net operating income.
iv) Select the most appropriate method of calculating the rate of return on investment and find out the rate that the market is looking for.
v) Estimate the market value by capitalization of the net income. That is, divide the net operating income by the capitalization rate.

The income approach is most often used with income generating properties, such as a commercial plaza or rental apartments (the whole building). Although it is common to rent out a house and income is then generated, the rate of return is usually low and it is difficult to sell a 'home' based on the income produced. As a result, the income approach is not always used in the evaluation of a house.

Following is a simple example to show how to estimate the value of an income-producing property.

Example

Assume the market is looking for a return rate of 10% (the capitalization rate).

i) Estimate of potential annual gross income = $140,000
ii) Deduct allowance for vacancy and bad debts (say 8%) $11,200 (-)
iii) Effective gross income = $128,800
iv) Deduct annual operating expenses $ 60,800 (-)
v) Net operating income before debt (NIBD) = $ 60,000

The estimated value of the property

= Net Operating Income Before Debt ÷ Capitalization Rate
= NIBD ÷ 10%
= $60,000 ÷ 10%
= $600,000

The Cost Approach

The cost approach is directly related to the principle of substitution in that a property's value is determined by the cost of acquiring an equally desirable property. The four basic steps to the cost approach are:

i) Estimate the land value as if vacant.
ii) Estimate the reproduction (or replacement) cost new of the improvements. That is, to calculate the cost to build a new building that is exactly the same as the subject property.
iii) Learn the life span of every improvement on the land; we do not have to deal with the land, as it lasts forever. Then learn their effective ages. The effective life of an improvement may be different from its chronological age

(actual age). If the improvement has had better than average maintenance, its effective age may be less than its actual age. If there has been inadequate maintenance, the effective age may be greater than the actual age.

iv) Estimate the depreciated value of the improvements from all causes.

v) Add the land value to the depreciated value of the improvements to obtain the final estimate of value by this approach.

The cost approach is most often used with new construction or is found effective in newer buildings. The effect of age causes forms of depreciation, which must be measured, which becomes a subjective exercise, often providing results that are less than meaningful. A house does not necessarily reflect the value that has a real relationship to cost. In consideration of all of the above, the cost approach is only for reference. The following example shows the simple way to estimate value by the cost approach.

Example

To estimate the value of a 3,200 -square-foot house by the cost approach, the following calculations were made:

i) Land value: $160,000.00*

ii) Improvements on land

The house

Cost for new construction
= Size (sq ft) x construction cost*
= 3,200 x $81.00
= $259,200.00

Life span: 60
Effective age: 7

Other Improvements

Cost of interior upgrades = $10,000.00
Life span: 60   Effective age: 3

Cost of central air and central vacuum = $4,000.00
Life span: 20   Effective age: 10

Cost of window coverings = $2,000.00
Life span: 60   Effective age: 7

Cost of the Finished Basement = $24,000.00
Life span: 60   Effective age: 8

iii) Calculate the depreciation.

The depreciated value of the house

= $259,200.00 x (60-7) ÷ 60 = $228,960.00

The depreciated values of other improvements

Interior upgrades = $10,000.00 × (60-3) ÷ 60
= $9,500.00

Central air and central vacuum
= $4,000.00 × (20-10) ÷ 20
= $2,000.00

Window coverings = $2,000.00 × (60-7) ÷ 60
= $1,766.66

Finished basement = $24,000.00 × (60-8) ÷ 60
= $20,800.00

Total = $34,066.66

<u>Total depreciated values of improvements</u>

= $228,960.00 + $9,500.00 + $2,000.00 + $1,766.66
 + $20,800.00

= $263,026.66

iv) Add the land value of $160,000 to the depreciated value

= $263,026.66 + $160,000.00

Indicated value by cost approach is: $423,026.66

Therefore, the appraised value by using the cost approach is $423,000.00 (rounded).

*It is hard for a person without appraising background to look for those data in order to perform a cost approach to value appraisal.

The Direct Sales Comparison Approach

This is the approach best understood by the public and reflects the interaction of the typical buyer and seller in the market place. This approach is founded on the principle of substitution, which states that a prudent buyer will pay no more for a property than it will cost to acquire an equally desirable substitute. This approach involves the gathering, analyzing, and comparing of data of similar properties that were sold, and adjusting the price for similarities and dissimilarities found in the properties. Adjustments are made to equalize differences between the comparables and the subject. Adjustments are made as they relate to components such as time, location, motivation, and physical conditions.

All adjustments are based on the price that a prudent buyer is willing to pay for the feature, but not the replacement cost of the item. For example, a new in-ground swimming pool can cost more than $10,000, but some buyers will not treat it as a benefit for most of the houses. As a result, sometimes we will make a very little adjustment on a swimming pool or even make a negative adjustment (adverse effect) for those areas where the weather is comparatively cold, as in New York.

Steps required

- Locate and select all available comparable sales and listings. Look for three to four primary qualities in selecting a good comparable sale;
- Within the local market area;
- At or near the date of the appraisal;
- Truly comparable, in that it will appeal to the same type of buyer who would consider buying the subject property

being appraised, e.g., if the appraisal is for a single-family home, then a duplex would not normally be a good comparable; and

- A bona fide arm's length transaction.

Based on the selections made, the appraiser would:

- Collect pertinent information on each comparable to make meaningful adjustments and gain a true understanding of the comparable properties. Direct inspection of comparables is an advantage in that regard.
- Analyze all relevant data, including differences between the comparable and subject, e.g., time of sale and features.
- Compare each property with the subject property, making the necessary adjustments. Adjustments can be either dollar amounts or percentages. Real estate practitioners typically use dollar adjustments.
- Reconcile the data and arrive at a reasonable value estimate.

An example is illustrated on the next pages.

DIRECT SALES COMPARISON APPROACH TO VALUE

Comparable Sales Adjustment Table

Comparable	Subject Property	Comparable One	Comparable Two	Comparable Three
Selling Price	---	$394,000.00	$410,000.00	$418,000.00
Time	9-May-03	12-Dec-02	30-Jan-03	2-May-03
Location	Ordinary	Ordinary	Ordinary	Ordinary
Lot Size	41'	41'	42'	41'
Type	2 Story	2 Story	2 Story	2 Story
Quality	Ordinary	Ordinary	Ordinary	Ordinary
Building size	3,200 sq ft	3,000 sq ft	3,200 sq ft	2,900 sq ft
Condition	Ordinary	Ordinary	Ordinary	Ordinary
Bathrooms	2x5 1x3 1x2	3x4 1x2	2x4 1x2	2x4 1x3 1x2
Garage	Double Attached	Double Attached	Double Attached	Double Attached
Basement	Finished	Unfinished	Unfinished	Finished
Special	Fireplace	Fireplace	Fireplace	Fireplace
	French Doors	4 appliances	4 appliances	5 appliances
	Window Blinds	Window Blinds	Window Blinds	Window Blinds
	Central Air	Central Vacuum	Central Air	Central Air
	Central Vacuum	Interlocking brick	Central Vacuum	Central Vacuum
	Parquet Floor	patio, walkway	9' Ceiling on G/F	Parquet Floor
	Enclosed Porch	& driveway		Water Softener
	Interlocking brick walkway & patio			Enclosed Porch

Comparable Sales Adjustment Chart

Comparable	Subject Property	Comparable One	Comparable Two	Comparable Three
Selling Price	---	$394,000	$410,000	$418,000
Time	---	$13,333	$13,333	$0

Location	---	$0	$0	$0
Lot Size	---	$0	$0	$0
Type	---	$0	$0	$0
Quality	---	$0	$0	$0
Building size	---	$10,000	$0	$15,000
Condition	---	$0	$0	$0
Bath Rooms	---	$500	$2,000	$1,000
Garage	---	$0	$0	$0
Basement	---	$10,000	$10,000	$0
Special	---	$4,000	$3,000	$500
Total Adjustment	---	$37,833	$28,333	$16,500
Adjusted Price	---	$431,833	$438,333	$434,500

Reconciliation

The adjusted sale prices range from $431,833 to $438,333. Comparable Three was the most recent sale and required the least adjustment. It was given the greatest weight.

The final estimate of value by the direct sales comparison approach is $435,000 (rounded).

Explanation of adjustment:

All adjustments are based on the price that a prudent buyer is willing to pay for the feature, but not the replacement cost of the item. For example, a new in-ground swimming pool can cost more than $10,000, but most buyers will not treat it as a benefit for most of the houses. As a result, a very little adjustment will be made to a swimming pool or even a negative adjustment (adverse effect) will be made.

Time

> Since there is a significant difference between the price in May 2003 and the prices in Jan 2003 and Dec 2002, it is reasonable to adjust the price of comparables 1 and 2 by $13,333. No adjustment was made on comparable 3.

Location

> Locations with negative effects, such as near main street, for houses like these, and with positive effects, such as backing onto woods, will be adjusted accordingly. No adjustment was made for all comparables.

Lot size

> No adjustment was made for all comparables, as there was no significant difference in lot sizes.

Type

> If the comparables are different types of properties, such as a two-story home and bungalow; adjustment will be made accordingly. No adjustment was made for all comparables.

Construction quality

> Both the quality of the material used and workmanship will affect the price. No adjustment was made for all comparables.

Building size

The adjustment is based on how much a buyer is willing to pay for the difference, not the building cost of the size. The usable areas of comparables one and three were significantly less than the subject; $10,000 and $15,000 were the adjustments, respectively.

Condition

The subject property is compared with the others; superior condition will have a positive adjustment and vice versa. No adjustment was made for all comparables.

Bathrooms

Adjustments were made according to the number of bathrooms and number of pieces inside the rooms.

Garage

All the garages were the same. No adjustment was made for all comparables.

Basement

The adjustment is based on the buyer's willingness to pay, but not the building cost. Comparables one and two had an unfinished basement; $10,000 was adjusted.

Specials

Items such as appliances, upgrades, fireplace, floorings and the central vacuum will be adjusted accordingly.

Evaluate Property Before Buying

Although it is difficult for a person who has no background in real estate to appraise houses, and it is not recommended to appraise your own home even if you are a professional appraiser, it is a good idea to give yourself a 'second opinion' by evaluating the house that you are going to buy. I am not saying you can appraise the house by yourself, but just try to evaluate it for your own consideration before submitting an offer to buy.

Before you commit to a purchase, you should try to evaluate the property by using the methods above, maybe with the assistance of your real estate agent. You then can have an idea of the market value of the house so that you will not pay too much. It is particularly useful when someone artificially inflates the price of a house and tries to sell it to you (the so-called illegal flipping); in which case the seller often cooperates with an appraiser to supply an appraisal much higher than the market value. Basic knowledge of appraising can help you avoid such scams.

It is especially useful if you are going to buy an investment property and are using the Income Approach to estimate the value. You may find the annual property operating data form in Appendix A useful.

Limitations

Even professional appraisers encounter limitations in appraising properties. Those limitations, of course, are also yours when you try to appraise properties yourself. We can list the limitations as follows:

    a)   We do not know if title to the property is good and marketable;

b) We do not know if there is encroachment, encumbrance, restriction, lease or covenant that would in any way affect the valuation, except as expressly noted in the documents we have;

c) We have to assume the existing use is a legally conforming use which may be continued by any buyer from the existing owner;

d) We have to assume that any rights of way, easements or encroachments over other real properties and leases or other covenants are legally enforceable.

e) Since we are not qualified surveyors and if no legal survey concerning the subject property has been provided, it is hard to know if there is any encroachment on the property.

f) We have to assume that there are no patent and latent defects in the property and that no banned materials such as urea formaldehyde foam are present.

g) We have to assume that the property is structurally sound and in need of no immediate repairs.

h) Since no soil tests have been done, we assume that there is no environmental problem with the property.

i) Unless an inspection was done, we assume the heating, plumbing, electrical, air conditioning or other systems are in good working order.

j) We assume the property has met all requirements of the local zoning office, the fire department, the building inspector, the health department or any other government regulatory agency. The subject property must comply with such government regulations. If it does not comply, its non-compliance may affect market value. To be certain of compliance, further investigations may be necessary.

k) We assume all data collected from the local land registry office or real estate board is correct, updated and full.

l) As well as using such documented and generally reliable evidence of market transactions, it is also necessary to rely on hearsay evidence.

m) Because market conditions, including economic, social and political factors, change rapidly and on occasion without warning, the market value expressed as of the date of this appraisal cannot be relied upon to estimate the market value as of any other date.

Market Information

You may collect market information from your real estate agents or local clerk office. It is very important to obtain accurate market information when performing an appraisal, even for simple evaluation. Although the approaches we use depend mainly on the history (for direct sales comparison approach) and present market data (both the income approach and cost approach), it is necessary to take the market trend (future performance) into consideration.

Professional appraisers will act more conservatively if the market is in the late expansion phase, which means prices are nearly at the peak. Usually, a three-month forecast will be done to lower the risk of over evaluation.

8. The Sources of Your Down Payment

Convert Your Assets

In order to fulfill the dream of owning a real property or the dream of being a landlord, you may need a decent down payment if you are not qualified for the 'no down payment' criteria. Consider selling some of your assets, like stocks, mutual funds and bonds.

Instead of leasing a new car to show off, consider keeping your old one and use the money to buy a house. For a monthly payment of $300, you can either lease a compact car or increase your mortgage amount by $100,000 under a mortgage rate of 6 percent. You may have to sacrifice other opportunities in order to fulfill the dream of owning real properties. The idea should be to buy yourself a nice car after you have earned enough money from real estate. You should keep in mind that a real estate is a tool of investment, while a car is a consumer product and will depreciate rapidly.

Add Up Small Savings

Investing in real estate can be a long-term project before the actual purchase. Saving the down payment is one of the most difficult hurdles. Do not overlook small savings, small amounts of money carefully saved can quickly add up to large amounts to use as a down payment.

Did you know that of the 400 billion cups of coffee consumed each year worldwide, the United States consumes one third? There are about 100 million coffee drinkers in the United States. It is fair to say that on average a coffee drinker drinks about 1,333 cups of coffee every year. This represents more than three cups a day. If you are a coffee drinker you probably drink more, as three-cup is only an average figure that includes occasional coffee consumers. Say you drink four cups every day and two of them were bought in coffee shops. You can save $2 a day by storing your own coffee in a Thermos and bringing it to work, or brewing your coffee in your workplace and sharing the costs with your colleagues. This can save you more than $500 that you would spend by buying coffees in cafes.

You can try using a saving bank (the best one is the old ceramic piggy bank) to save money. Every day, put at least two dollars, or all the coins in your pocket into it; whichever is more. At the end of the year, put all the money saved into your saving account, opened for the sole purpose of buying a home. This could save you more than $700 a year. It works.

Part-Time Job

My friend John worked for an engineering firm for three years after the completion of his university education. He earned $50,000 a year and lived by himself, but he had no money left in his pocket, not even a penny. In fact, he used the cash advance service provided by credit card companies to pay for his spending: vacations, a nice car, a home theatre set and all the luxuries. He knew it would lead him to bankruptcy sooner or later, but it was hard for him to change those spending habits. I suggested he find a part-time job and work both at nights and weekends. He did and ultimately paid off all his debts in two years.

The benefit from a part-time job is more than earning extra money for you; you will have less chance to spend money too. If your part-time job earns you $100 a week after tax, you may save more than $200 a week, as you will not have the time to spend. You may save over $10,000 a year; your down payment can then easily be saved.

Money from the Others

You may not be able to save the down payment within a short period. If the market is at the peak you will not mind waiting a couple of years more, as the price will go down after a period of time. If the market is at a low level, then you may not want to miss a good chance to buy property at a good price.

You may use other people's money, from your parents, siblings, relatives or friends. You may be able to borrow money from them at a very low-interest rate or even at no interest. Try to divide the money you need in small amounts so that everyone can afford to lend it to you. For example, you need $10,000 as a down payment; then you should divide the $10,000 into $500 portions. Asking people to lend you $500 is much easier than asking them to lend you $1,000 or more. Moreover, people will seldom ask for interest for a $500 loan. Nevertheless, you should try your best to pay back such loans to them as they are your assets and you may need their assistance in the future. Good reputation and credit history are always your number-one priorities.

There are many ways to use other people's money to buy real estate. The problem is you cannot use them twice. For example, you may ask your parents to 'sponsor' you in buying a house to live in, but what about buying an investment property? People are willing to assist you to establish your own home, but may not be willing to help you invest. So use your money wisely.

The 'Cheating' Clause

Some people intentionally will make use of an incorrectly drafted financing clause to get more than 100 percent of a financing fund. They ask the seller to take back a second mortgage and at the same time increase the amount on the first mortgage. For example, you state in the offer that you were going to arrange a 50 percent first mortgage from your bank and asked the seller to take back a second mortgage at 30 percent of the purchase price. The seller agreed, but before closing the deal, you successfully asked your bank to increase its mortgage to 80 percent. The total loan borrowed was then 110 percent of the purchase price. It meant you would get a 'cash bonus' equal to 10 percent of the purchase price.

Originally, when we use a financing clause, the wording will like this:

*This Offer is conditional upon the Buyer arranging, at the Buyer's own expense, a new first mortgage for **not less than** One Hundred Thousand Dollars ($100,000), amortized over 30 years, bearing interest at a rate of not more than 7% per annum, repayable in blended monthly payments of about Six Hundred Sixty Five Dollars and Thirty One Cents ($665.31), including principal and interest, and to run for a term of not less than five years from the date of completion of this transaction. Unless the Buyer gives notice in writing delivered to the Seller not later than 5:00 p.m. on the 14th day of February 2019, that this condition is fulfilled, this Offer shall be null and void and the deposit shall be returned to the Buyer in full without deduction. This condition is included for the benefit of the Buyer and may be waived at the Buyer's sole option by notice in writing to the Seller within the time period stated herein.*

However, if it is used together with a seller-take-back mortgage, it should be reworded so that the seller can make sure the buyer will not over-finance the property hence protect herself/himself. Actually, it is very simple to do that. All we need is to change the word 'less' to 'more' so that the whole clause has a different meaning:

*This Offer is conditional upon the Buyer arranging, at the Buyer's own expense, a new first mortgage for **not more than** One Hundred Thousand Dollars ($100,000), amortized over 30 years, bearing interest at a rate of not more than 7% per annum, repayable in blended monthly payments of about Six Hundred Sixty Five Dollars and Thirty One Cents ($665.31), including principal and interest, and to run for a term of not less than five years from the date of completion of this transaction. Unless the Buyer gives notice in writing delivered to the Seller not later than 5:00 p.m. on the 14th day of February 2019, that this condition is fulfilled, this Offer shall be null and void and the deposit shall be returned to the Buyer in full without deduction. This condition is included for the benefit of the Buyer and may be waived at the Buyer's sole option by notice in writing to the Seller within the time period stated herein.*

Under such a clause, the buyer has the obligation NOT to arrange a first mortgage of more than $100,000. As a result, the seller's second mortgage is protected, as the combined mortgage loan of the first mortgage and the seller-take-back (second mortgage) will not be more than the preset amount.

Some people will have the financing clauses prepared using the first clause (with the words 'not less than') when the seller is taking back a second mortgage. By doing so, they can easily arrange 100 percent financing, or even more, by raising the percentage of the first mortgage.

As a buyer, you can also arrange a third mortgage in addition to the two mortgages mentioned in the offer without getting the consent from the bank or the seller. The reason is that the arrangement of a third mortgage, even if the total loan is more than 100 percent, will not affect the redeemable equity of the first and second mortgages.

104 Percent Financing

Some private lenders and small financial companies will offer 100 percent financing to homebuyers. That is, you do not need to pay any down payment. Since providing 100 percent financing will involve higher risks, those lenders will require a strong credit history and a stable job with high income. Moreover, they will charge an up-front fee (the private mortgage insurance fee) up to 4 percent of the purchase price of your home. This results in the same problem as not having enough money for a down payment. Some lenders will incorporate such a fee in the lending fund and amortize it over thirty years.

For example, the purchase price of your home is $100,000, and you ask for a 100 percent financing plan. The lender will lend you $100,000 to pay for the house, but the mortgage amount will be $104,000 instead of $100,000, as the 4% administration fee is included in the mortgage loan. Again, traditional methods (calculating your ETI and DTI) will be used to determine if you are eligible for such a loan.

Buying Landlord's House

If you are renting a house, you may wish to buy the house from your landlord. Buying the house you are living in from your landlord has several benefits. First, since you have been living there for a while you should know the neighbourhood well and know if it is the one you want. Second, you know if there is any problem with the house. In fact, you know it better than your landlord does. Third, your landlord may sell the house to you at a price lower than fair market value when there is no real estate agent involved and the landlord is not well informed of the market performance.

Most importantly, you are much more likely to get a seller-take-back mortgage from your landlord than from other sellers. Your landlord knows you well for the payment history; s/he will not worry that her/his mortgage will be in default if you have been paying her/him the rent on time. Moreover, most landlords will not use the ETI and DTI when approving your mortgage request, and they may charge a lower private mortgage insurance premium as compared to other private lenders. As a result, you have a higher success rate in getting a seller-take-back mortgage than obtaining a mortgage somewhere else.

9. Option to Buy

Option and First Right of Refusal

To many stock investors, an option is a familiar term. Simply speaking, an option in the stock market is the privilege of buying a specified amount of a specified stock at a specified price within a specified time. Similarly, an option (to buy) in real estate an owner grants an investor the privilege to buy a certain property within a specified time at a specified price.

The option to buy gives the buyer the right to buy but does not impose any obligation to do so. If the option is not exercised, the contract will end. The cost of a real estate option ranges from a few hundred dollars to over tens of thousand dollars. It depends upon the value of the property and the holding period of the option. An option to buy is normally not used in residential transactions but would apply in transactions dealing with industrial, commercial and investment properties. However, you may use an option to buy in homes and vacant lands if you are a flipper (people who flip properties). An option to buy is the best speculative tool as it gives flippers the greatest leverage.

The first right of refusal, commonly used in a lease, has a similar effect as an option. The first right of refusal is usually a provision in a lease that gives a tenant the privilege to buy the rented property or to rent the space adjacent to the rented property upon a certain event, such as the landlord accepting a written offer to sell the rented property, or the vacating of the adjacent property. When the first right of refusal involves buying the rented property, terms and conditions of the sale offered the tenant must be the same as those given the third party in the accepted offer. In this sense, the first right of refusal cannot be used as an investment tool since it is a passive clause that will come into effect only when the landlord wishes to sell the property and eventually has an accepted offer. Moreover, instead of a pre-fixed price in an option to buy, the sale price of the first right of refusal is to be determined by the accepted offer made by a third party. Therefore, the chance to make a profit from it is very low.

Flipping Lands

My friend Michael in Illinois once told me one of his success stories regarding increasing the value of land. Like me, he was a commercial real estate consultant and was approached by his friend one day for a real estate problem. His friend owned a piece of land and received a letter from the state government advising her that it was going to expropriate her land for highway construction. The government agreed to pay her $200,000 as compensation, and she wanted to seek a second opinion, although she felt that $200,000 was already higher than what she thought the land was worth.

That was ten acres of junk land, storing dumped cars and furniture. The owner had always worried about the problem of contamination, as some of the cars were leaking oil. That was the reason she felt $200,000 was already a good price to get rid of it. After studying the case, my friend sent out marketing packages to eight automobile companies to invite them to open a new dealership there. Six out of eight showed interest, and finally, four of them actually made proposals to buy the land. Among the four proposals received, the lowest price was $2.5 million and the top price was $3.5 million. As a result, the owner received $2 million in compensation from the government instead of $200,000. That was a 900 percent increase, and my friend, of course, received a decent commission.

This is one of the thousands of cases in which land value can soar several times above its 'original' price. This also explains why some people are so crazy about flipping land. As I said before, many real estate professionals discourage people from flipping, as it is risky for those who have little knowledge of real estate. However, if you really want to flip real properties, using an option is one of the best methods.

Unlike buying a real property, buying an option involves no soft cost, no mortgage and no significant down payment (not until you exercise the option). The liability of the buyer is the money paid for the option and nothing more. For example, if you bought a real property for $400,000 and flipped it for $420,000, you might realize a loss instead of a gain. Such probable loss is due to the commission you must pay for the sale of the property and the soft cost paid when you bought it. With a few thousand dollars, you probably can buy an option on a piece of land worth more than $400,000 and with a potential to grow much more than $20,000.

A real estate option gives speculators flexibility and control of the property. When the real estate market goes up, the speculator can exercise her/his option to buy the property and flip it for a big profit. Speculators will usually target vacant lands (farmlands and junk lands) since the increase in value is usually significant when the land is developed. Moreover, since landowners may have nothing to do with the lands, they are more willing to accept an option than a building owner is. By investing a few thousand dollars and having the potential to flip the property, for say, half a million dollars, an option is a wheel of fortune to many speculators.

My friend Cliff used $6,000 to buy an option on a piece of land with a value of more than $1 million; he sold his option in three months and earned more than $100,000. Such investments, however, involve professional knowledge of land use and are not suitable for ordinary investors.

Option in a Lease

Besides a tool for speculation, an option to buy sometimes provides a 'try before buying' alternative to tenants. A landlord will include an option to buy clause in the lease so that the tenant may have the right to buy the real property within the term of the lease for a preset price. The main difference between a first right of refusal to buy and an option to buy in a lease is that there is no preset price in the first right of refusal and the holder can exercise it only when the seller has an accepted agreement of purchase and sale, while the price in an option to buy is preset and the holder can exercise it at any time before the option expires.

A typical option to buy clause in a lease may look like this:

In consideration of the Tenant to enter this lease agreement with the Landlord, and in consideration of the terms and conditions herein recited, the Landlord gives to the Tenant an option irrevocable within the time limit herein for acceptance, to buy, free and clear of all encumbrances, the lands and premises referred to in the Agreement of Purchase and Sale attached hereto and initialed by the parties for identification. The option shall be open for acceptance by notice in writing delivered to the Landlord not later than 5:00 p.m. on the 12th day of December 2005. The terms of the purchase shall be the Agreement of Purchase and Sale attached hereto

An agreement of purchase and sale with the agreed terms and conditions has to be attached to the lease and initialled by both parties. A sample option to buy and a sample of agreement of purchase and sale are printed as Appendix D and E for your reference.

If you want to include an Option to Buy clause in your lease, you should consult your legal counsel or a competent real estate agent to assist you in drafting the clause.

10. Arranging the Agreement

Although a professional real estate agent can assist you in drafting your offer to buy, the following sections can give you an idea of the meaning of important clauses to protect yourself in case you do not have a real estate agent to represent you. However, you are reminded and it is strongly recommended that legal advice should be sought before drafting your own offer.

Setting the Price

We are told that we should not make the first offer in any negotiation. When a house is for sale, it must have an asking price. Therefore, do not be afraid to offer the seller a price since the seller has already offered you her/his asking price.

Some buyers will offer a price well below the market price to test the water. Although using such a technique has a higher chance to buy a property at a low price, you also have a higher chance of failing. As a result, it may take you a much longer time in your buying process.

The Irrevocable Time

When a buyer drafts an offer, s/he has to tell the seller the irrevocable time. It is the period of time that the buyer (or the person who makes an offer) leaves the offer open for consideration by the seller (or the person who receives the offer). In other words, s/he cannot withdraw her/his offer until the end of the stated time period. If the seller accepts her/his offer within the irrevocable time, the offer will then become an agreement.

When you, as a buyer, make an offer to a seller for

consideration, the wording you should use is:

> *This Offer shall be irrevocable by the Buyer until 5:00 p.m. on the 15th day of November 2004. If this offer is not accepted by the other party after that time, it shall be null and void and the deposit shall be returned to the Buyer in full without any deduction or interest.*

If the seller makes a counteroffer to you, then it shall be irrevocable by the seller and change the time if needed. Use caution when setting the irrevocable time. Some people will attempt to keep the irrevocable time extremely short to impose an inordinate amount of pressure on the other party. You may use this tactic if you like, but you should also know how to deal with it when you are presented with such an offer.

The Deposit

There is confusion between a deposit and a consideration. A consideration is something of value given or promised to make an agreement legally binding; it can be money or any goods. In common law, when a promise is made under seal, no consideration is required since the law presumes that the solemn act of sealing replaces consideration. Nowadays in real estate, almost all agreements are signed under seal (by using a sticker or a small black dot pre-printed on the form as the seal) and therefore there is always a consideration in the agreement even the buyer pays no deposit.

A deposit is, in fact, not a necessary part of an offer. In buying real estate, it is used as a good faith effort to show the seller how serious the buyer is. It can be any amount as long as it is acceptable by the seller. A buyer will give a higher deposit if s/he wants to show the seller that s/he is very serious in buying the seller's home. On the other hand, if a buyer has no down payment, s/he will submit a deposit as little as a few hundred dollars, or even no deposit at all. Moreover, you may wish to pay the deposit only after you have learned that all the conditions in the offer are fulfilled.

Following is a sample clause used to pay the deposit after satisfying all conditions:

> *The Buyer agrees to pay a sum of Three Thousand Dollars ($3,000.00), to the seller's agent, by negotiable check, at the time of notification of fulfillment or removal of all the conditions stated herein, as a deposit to be held in trust pending completion or other termination of this Agreement. This amount is to be credited towards the purchase price on completion of this transaction.*

You should ask for interest on your deposit if the amount is significant and the closing date is more than thirty days from the date of submitting your offer (or from the date upon waiving all conditions). A clause like this may help:

> *Both the Buyer and the Seller hereby direct the Seller's Agent to place same in an interest-bearing account or term deposit, with any accrued interest on the deposit to be paid to the Buyer as soon as possible after completion or other termination of this Agreement. In case the closing date is advanced or in the event that this Agreement is terminated, the Buyer agrees to accept the short-term rate for deposits withdrawn before maturity*

Right to Assign

It is always a good idea to include a clause in your offer that grants you the right to assign the agreement to a third party. By doing so, you will have the right to sell the property (transfer the agreement) to a third party before the closing date. That is, you have the chance to flip.

> *It is understood and agreed between the Parties that the Buyer shall have the right at any time prior to closing, to assign this Agreement to an individual, persons, a partnership or a company, either existing or to be incorporated, without the consent of the Seller. Upon delivery to the Seller of notice of such assignment, together with the assignee's covenant in favour of the Seller to be bound hereby as Buyer, the Buyer hereinbefore named shall stand released from all further liability hereunder.*

The Financing Clause (Mortgage Contingency Clause)

A financing clause (or sometimes called a mortgage contingency clause) is a provision in the buying contract that allows the buyer to call the whole deal off if s/he cannot arrange a mortgage within a fixed period of time. In other words, although the offer is accepted by both parties, it is still conditional on the buyer being able to obtain a mortgage on the property. Usually, the buyer will specify what kind of mortgage(s) s/he needs in order to let the seller know the feasibility of obtaining that kind of mortgage(s). That is, the clause will specify the mortgage rate, term, amortization, amount of the mortgage to be arranged and the amount of monthly payment (like the one we used in Chapter 8, The Cheating Clause). However, you, as a buyer, may find the following clause to be more practical and provide you more protection.

> *THIS OFFER IS CONDITIONAL upon the Buyer arranging, at his own expense, a new First Mortgage that is <u>satisfactory</u> to him. Unless the Buyer gives notice in writing delivered to the Seller by 11:59 p.m. on the 5th business day after the acceptance of this offer,*

> that this condition is fulfilled, this Offer shall be null and void and the deposit shall be returned to the Buyer in full without interest. This condition is included for the <u>sole benefit of the Buyer</u> and may be waived at his option by notice in writing to the Seller within the time period stated herein.

By using the word **satisfactory**, you could simplify the lengthy wording to describe the details of the mortgage and save effort in calculating the payment (like the one we used in the 'cheating' clause). However, it does not provide an escape for you in case you change your mind and do not want to proceed with the sale.

The reason is that the word 'satisfactory' means satisfactory to a reasonable person with all the subjective but reasonable standards of the particular buyer. That is, you are supposed to use your best efforts to obtain financing that is satisfactory to you, and you are not to withhold your satisfaction unreasonably.

Moreover, the words "sole benefit of the buyer" does not release the buyer from the duty to make his best efforts to seek "satisfactory financing."

Seller-Take-Back Clause

When you want to ask the seller to take back a mortgage, you may use a clause like this:

> The Seller agrees to take back a second mortgage in the amount of Fifty Thousand Dollars ($50,000.00), bearing interest at the rate of 6% per annum, amortized over 30 years, repayable in blended monthly payments of Two Hundred Ninety Nine Dollars and

> *Seventy Eight Cents ($299.78), including both principal and interest, and to run for a term of Five (5) years from the date of completion of this transaction. This mortgage shall contain a clause permitting the mortgagor, when not in default, the privilege of prepaying all or part of the principal sum outstanding at any time or times without notice or bonus. This mortgage shall also contain a clause permitting the mortgagor, when not in default, the privilege of renewing this mortgage on its maturity, for a further term of Five (5) years on the same terms and conditions.*

The above clause consists of the 'seller take back' clause, the prepayment privilege and the renewal privilege. As there is no limit in the prepayment privilege, it is actually an open mortgage. Moreover, the renewal privilege is a 'looping' clause in that the renewal privilege will stay there every time the mortgage is renewed. That is, the mortgage will be renewed until the end of the amortization period or in the event, the buyer wants to pay back the mortgage in full.

The Survey Clause

The survey of a freehold property can show if there is any problem with respect to the building, such as encroachment and set-back requirements stipulated by local authorities. Having an out-of-date survey is no better than having no survey at all, as an out-of-date survey might be taken before the reconstruction of the property. To request an up-to-date survey is a good idea, but the word 'up-to-date' is an arguable term, as an up-to-date survey may mean the survey was taken just before the closing date. As a result, many sellers or their agents will change the word 'up-to-date' to 'existing'. However, such a change will bring the problem back to square one since an existing survey may already be out-of-date.

The following clause may solve this problem. In this clause, the buyer asks for title insurance (one-time premium insurance for the property owner to make sure there is no problem in getting a good and clear title) to replace a survey if the survey is an unacceptable one or the seller cannot produce one.

The cost of title insurance, often set by state insurance commissions, can vary widely state to state. The cost can be over $800 in some states, while people can buy it for just $150 on the same kind of property in other states. Buying title insurance, in fact, is a better alternative than to ask for a survey, since title insurance provides better protection than having an accurate and up-to-date survey.

> *Seller hereby agrees to provide at her/his expense to the Buyer within 3 days following acceptance of this offer, with a copy of an existing survey. If there is no survey available from the Seller or the survey provided is not acceptable to the Buyer's lawyer or lender, then the Seller hereby agrees to pay the cost of placing a policy of title insurance on the subject property on or before the closing date.*

Such clause should be used together with a financing clause so if there is any problem with the survey, the lender will let you know and you may choose to end the agreement by using the financing clause.

The Financial Statement Clause

If you buy a condo unit it is important to know the building corporation is in a sound financial background. A clause like this may protect you from buying a unit in a problem building.

> Seller hereby agrees to deliver the most current financial statement of the corporation of the subject condo building, at Sellers cost, to the Buyer's lawyer within five business days after the acceptance of this Offer. THIS OFFER IS THEN CONDITIONAL upon the approval of such a financing statement by the Buyer's lawyer and the result is satisfactory to her/him. Unless the Buyer gives notice in writing delivered to the Seller by 11:59 p.m. on the 3rd business day after the receipt of the financial statement, that this condition is fulfilled, this Offer shall be null and void and the deposit shall be returned to the Buyer in full without interest. This condition is included for the sole benefit of the Buyer and may be waived at her/his option by notice in writing to the Seller within the time period stated herein.

The Inspection Clause

Adding an inspection clause can protect you from buying a house with structural problems or major deficiency. A typical inspection clause may look like this:

> THIS OFFER IS CONDITIONAL upon the inspection of the subject property by a registered (certified) home inspector by 11:59 p.m. on the 5th business day after the acceptance of this offer and the obtaining of a report which is satisfactory to him. In the event such inspection reveals a deficiency in the subject property which the Buyer is unwilling to accept or which the Seller is unable or unwilling to remedy, then this Offer shall be null and void and the deposit shall be returned to the Buyer in full without interest. The Seller agrees to cooperate in providing access to the structure for the purpose of this inspection. This condition is included for the sole benefit of the Buyer and may be waived at

> her/his option by notice in writing to the Seller within the time period stated herein.

Such a condition enables the buyer to declare the agreement null and void if there is something wrong with the house. Since no house is perfect, even new homes, people can easily point out the 'problems' to be fixed or improved, the buyer can make use of this condition to re-negotiate with the seller. In some cases, buyers did convince the sellers to take hundreds or thousands of dollars from the price they had agreed upon. As a result, more and more sellers are wary of this inspection clause.

A more reasonably drafted inspection clause may look like this:

> THIS OFFER IS CONDITIONAL upon the inspection of the subject property by a registered (certified) home inspector by 11:59 p.m. on the 5th business day after the acceptance of this offer and the obtaining of a report **showing no major and structural defect**. In the event the inspection reveals such deficiency in the subject property which the Buyer is unwilling to accept or which the Seller is unable or unwilling to remedy, then this Offer shall be null and void and the deposit shall be returned to the Buyer in full without interest The Seller agrees to cooperate in providing access to the structure for the purpose of this inspection. This condition is included for the sole benefit of the Buyer and may be waived at her/his option by notice in writing to the Seller within the time period stated herein.

Sellers will feel better if buyers can only declare the offer null and void for a major or structural defect. However, one will wonder how major the deficiency must be to cause the offer to be voided. As a result, another version of the inspection clause comes out:

THIS OFFER IS CONDITIONAL upon the inspection of the subject property by a registered (certified) home inspector by 11:59 p.m. on the 5th business day after the acceptance of this offer and the obtaining of a report showing no major and structural defect **that will cost more than $5,000 per single incidence to fix it**. *In the event the inspection reveals such deficiency in the subject property which the Buyer is unwilling to accept or which the Seller is unable or unwilling to remedy, then this Offer shall be null and void and the deposit shall be returned to the Buyer in full without interest. The Seller agrees to cooperate in providing access to the structure for the purpose of this inspection. This condition is included for the sole benefit of the Buyer and may be waived at her/his option by notice in writing to the Seller within the time period stated herein.*

This provides a guideline on how major a deficiency can be so that there will be no argument after signing the agreement. This is the fairest inspection clause to both the seller and the buyer.

Fixtures and Chattels

One of the most arguable subjects in a real estate transaction is the difference between fixtures and chattels. In general, an improvement or a personal property on the real property is a fixture when it is attached to the real property, either the building or the land. A chattel is, on the contrary, a moveable object that may be removed without injury to the real property. When we buy real estate, all the fixtures are included in the price, but not chattels. That is why it is necessary to distinguish them.

Furnace and air conditioning units are fixtures while picture frames and furniture are chattels. These are items that create no questions. How about an interlocking brick-paved patio? Is it attached to the land? The central vacuum is attached to the house, but not its hose and power head. Are they fixtures or chattels? A lawyer told me one of his clients took away all the light bulbs and fuses in the house he sold, claiming that they were chattels, as they were not attached to the house directly. This is, of course, an extreme case, and most people will not do that. However, it is a good practice to list 'equipment' that you want to stay with the house to avoid confusion.

It is also good to record the make, model and the serial number of the appliances if they are included in the purchase price of a house.

Possession

We will ask for vacant possession when we buy our homes. However, if it is an investment property, we might not wish the tenant to move out, because finding another tenant takes time and costs money. Even if you do not have to pay any commission in renting, if you rent out the house by yourself, the vacancy period costs you money too. If you want the existing tenant to stay in the property you are going to buy, make a request in the offer to assume the tenant and ask the seller not to inform the tenant without your consent. You then may assure yourself instant cash income in the first month of owning that house.

On the other hand, you may not know if the existing tenant is a good one or not. Maybe a bad tenant is the only reason the seller wants to sell the house — to get rid of the problem. Therefore, it may be a good idea to ask for vacant possession, even though the existing tenant is willing to stay. It protects you from assuming a trouble-making tenant.

If the house is vacant, you are more able to negotiate the deal. Holding a vacant house costs the seller, in general, over a thousand dollars a month. Assuming the house is worth $200,000. After the sale, the seller can put $200,000 in the bank to gain interest. If there is a mortgage on the house, the seller can save interest on the mortgage and gain interest on the balance after repaying the lender. More or less, it is the same case as if the seller has $200,000 in cash after the sale. A five percent (5%) term deposit interest on $200,000 can earn the seller $10,000 a year, which equals $833.33 a month.

If the seller sells the house one month later, that means s/he will earn one month interest less (or to pay one month more of mortgage interest). Adding the property tax s/he has to pay, one can fairly say that a one-month delay in selling would cost the seller more than one thousand dollars a month. If it is a condo unit, the 'loss' will be higher, as the seller has to pay a condo fee too.

You should present these figures to the seller and make your possession time as short as possible in order to request a lower price.

11. Working with Real Estate Agents

It is always a good idea to employ a competent real estate agent to assist you in trading real estate, especially when you are a buyer and do not have to pay the commission. However, when you engage an agency relationship with a real estate agent, you should know your rights and obligations before signing the agency agreement (or even before talking to them). Since real estate brokers and salespersons are licensed and regulated by local state laws, you may call the local authority for details or browse the websites of the state's real estate associations and local real estate boards for consumer information.

Although agency relationship can be an implied one under common law if there is no agency agreement signed between the broker and the consumer, some states do have statutes to override this rule. In those states (like New Mexico), a consumer who wants to create an agency relationship must sign a written agreement. If you use services provided by real estate agents in those states without an express written agency agreement, no agency relationship or agency duties will be imposed on that brokerage. That means you have no agent to represent your interest.

As most states still use agency law in a common law system to regulate real estate agents, the following sections are based on common law practice.

The Agent's Role

An agent is a person authorized by another person, known as the principal, to represent the principal in business transactions with a third party. In the real estate profession, it refers to a broker (a person or a company). In daily life, we call all real estate salespersons and brokers 'agents' or simply call them realtors. Realtor is, in fact, a registered trademark of the National Association of Realtors.

As a matter of law, a real estate agent who represents a principal (can be a seller, a buyer, a landlord or a tenant) owes that principal the highest duty of good faith; the agent must represent the principal's best interest at all times. The real estate agent also owes her/his principal duty of confidentiality regarding information about the principal.

There are mainly two types of agency relationships. Namely, a seller's agent (listing agent) and a buyer's agent (cooperating agent). When you sell your house, for example, the agent you employ is a seller's agent. When you want to buy or rent a real property, you will probably work with a buyer's agent.

In recent years, more and more real estate boards require their members to explain the agency relationships to their potential customers before signing any agreement. In the old days, there was an illusion among most consumers. People thought the agent working with a buyer was a buyer's agent. In fact, in most cases, the agent who worked for the buyer was the seller's agent. Since most real estate agents advertised their listing in the MLS system of their local real estate board, this created a sub-agency for the cooperating agent. On the other hand, the cooperating agent had an implied buyer's agency with the buyer, as there was no disclosure made by the buyer's agent stating that s/he was a sub-agent of the seller. Most buyers would then assume the agents who worked for them were buyer's agents. Conflicts of interest were created and some lawsuits were filed against agents.

To protect both the real estate agents and the general public, real estate agents are required to explain the agency relationship with their clients and get an agency agreement signed if possible. Several types of relationships may exist between a buyer and a cooperating agent in a real estate transaction:

Sub-agent of Seller

> When there is no agency relationship between the buyer and her/his agent disclosed to the seller, and if the listing is on an MLS system, there is an implied agency relationship between the seller and the buyer's agent. That is, the buyer's agent is, in fact, the sub-agent of the seller. Some buyers will sign a consent form with his agent to allow such sub-agent relationship to exist between the seller and buyer's agent instead of a buyer's agency relationship with the buyer. As a buyer, this type of agency relationship should be strongly discouraged, as you will not get the client service provided by your agent, and your best interest will not be protected.

Buyer's agent, compensated by the seller's agent

> This is the kind of agency relationship that most buyers will choose. Buyers get the utmost protection from this type of relationship. The commission is charged by the seller's agent, and s/he will pay a portion of it to the buyer's agent. As a result, the buyer does not have to pay any commission from his own pocket.

Buyer's agent, compensated by the buyer

> This kind of agency relationship is seldom used. People will use it when they do acquisitions on unlisted properties.

Dual agent

> When a real estate firm (not necessarily the same salesperson) represents both the seller and buyer, then a dual agency exists. The broker or her/his sales representative is called a dual agent. When a real estate agent acts as a dual agent, s/he can only provide limited confidentiality to her/his clients. The limited confidentially will prevent disclosure that the seller will accept a price less than the asking or listed price, that the buyer will pay a price greater than the price submitted in a written offer, of the motivation of any party for selling or buying property, that a seller or buyer will agree to financing terms other than those offered, or of any other information requested by a party to remain confidential. All other information is not treated confidentially.

Designated Agent

> A designated agent is a real estate agent who acts as the sole representative of a client. It is widely used in some states by brokers who want to avoid dual agencies. When a real estate salesperson is a designated agent of a buyer-client and there is another salesperson in the same office acting as a designated agent of a seller-client, there is no dual agency involved, as both agents are acting for only one client. However, the broker must maintain impartiality to both parties, and must not disclose confidential information of either party.

Non-Agent (Customer Status)

> A real estate salesperson can provide services to a consumer as a non-agent on an exclusive basis. This can

avoid the creation of a dual agency when the salesperson is acting as an agent for the seller and acting as a non-agent to the buyer. A written non-agency agreement is required to create this relationship.

It is similar to the case of a seller's subagent. The difference is there are two agents involved in the case of a seller's subagent; the cooperating agent is the seller's subagent. For a non-agent situation, there is only one agent involved, and s/he is the seller's agent and a non-agent of the buyer.

The Duties of an Agent

Some people feel that real estate agents are bloodsuckers who make their living by squeezing sellers and buyers. In fact, a professional real estate agent will not squeeze her/his client. On the contrary, s/he will fight for her/his client's best interest. Employing a good real estate agent is one of the keys to succeeding in trading real estate.

Many sellers complain about how aggressive their agents were, and how much they suffered from the selling prices. One thing many sellers seem to forget is that the listing agent is acting for the seller, thus s/he has an obligation of securing as high a price as can fairly be obtained. The same obligations apply to a buyer's agent when serving buyers. That is, to buy a property at a price as low as possible.

According to common law, an agent owes her/his principal several duties.

i. Good Faith

>An agent is required to place the interests of her/his

principal above all else except the law. When an agent has any personal interest, direct or indirect, in a real estate transaction, it is her/his strict duty to make full disclosure to her/his principal. The agent has to report to the principal all pertinent facts that could affect the judgment of an offer.

An agent may not make any secret profit other than the compensation agreed upon with her/his principal. For example, when a lender provides a referral fee (also called the founder's fee) to an agent who introduces her/his buyer to arrange a mortgage with that lender, it is necessary to have a clause in all her/his offers (or on a disclosure document), stating that a referral fee may be compensated by a lender and all the parties to that transact agree with it.

ii. Obedience

As a principal, you have the right to instruct your agent. An agent should then strictly follow the principal's lawful instructions.

Instructions such as not allowing showing appointments after 9 p.m., and requiring at least twenty-four hours notice for showing appointments are quite common when a seller sells her/his home.

iii. Competence

In representing the client, the agent must exercise a degree of care and skill that may be expected from an average practitioner in the real estate field. As a result, a newly licensed sales representative should not undertake a listing or serve a buyer alone. S/he should work with an experienced agent until s/he is competent to do so. Some brokerage firms require newly registered salespersons to work with an experienced partner for the first five transactions or the first six months.

Consequently, an agent specialized only in residential real estate should take over a commercial listing only with the assistance of a colleague who is specialized in the commercial field.

iv. Accounting

Real estate agents have to account for all funds. Money paid to a brokerage firm as a deposit for a property should be kept in a separate trust account so that the money is protected from any creditor's claim in case the brokerage firm goes bankrupt. As a buyer, make sure you write the check with the words 'in trust' after the name of the deposit holder (usually the listing broker).

Choosing the Right Agent

Real estate agents usually can assist buyers in three areas

i. Providing Market Information

Although most houses sold are in the MLS system and can be seen by visiting appropriate real estate websites, the information obtained from individual real estate agents is always the latest one. Some websites may list over 1 million homes for sale throughout the United States and provide links to real estate broker websites and a host of related realty services. However, there may be a delay in uploading the data from local real estate boards or individual brokers to those sites. As a result, sometimes when you find a listing on the Internet, the house has already been sold.

Some buyers like to shop properties by driving to the neighbourhood and looking for the 'For Sale' sign. Again, there may be a delay in installing the sign and the house may have been sold before the sign was erected. Moreover, some sellers may refuse erection of a 'For Sale' sign on their lawn, so you cannot tell if the house is for sale or not.

Hiring an agent to work for you can save time in searching and give you a higher chance of buying a good property.

ii. Market Value Evaluation

Since most real estate agents have been in some sort of training to evaluate residential properties, the value they estimate is quite close to the market value in most cases. The purpose of a market evaluation is to let the buyer know the market price of the home s/he is going to buy and to assure that s/he will not pay too much for it. If the offering price from the buyer is reasonable, a win-win situation for all parties can easily be achieved.

What is a reasonable price? It depends on the market, but certainly not the price at which the seller purchased the house. Who cares what the price of a house was in 1989 when all properties in North America soared to the highest level? On the other hand, you cannot expect a house to be sold to you at $200,000, although the seller bought it for $180,000 twenty years ago.

We often receive flyers from real estate agents saying that

a house was sold at 98 percent or at an even higher percentage of its asking price. Some buyers would say they did not buy that property because the sellers did not reduce their price low enough, as some sellers could reduce their prices by 10 percent or even more. We have to understand that the sale price of a house is based on its actual value, not a discount of its asking price.

If the asking price is low, then the sold price will be at a higher percentage of it. It can even exceed 100 percent of the asking price in some cases. If the asking price is high, then certainly the seller can give a big 'discount' to the buyer.

Remember, the seller can set her/his price at any level s/he wants. The final sale price is determined by its market value, but not a percentage of its asking price. You should ask your agent to print out the sale history of the houses in the same neighbourhood with similar features. You then will have a better comparison of prices and may use the direct sales comparison approach to estimate the price of the house you like.

iii. Offer Presentation

Although not all real estate agents are professionally trained in negotiation, most are excellent negotiators, especially the experienced ones. There are so many items to be negotiated in an offer presentation. Price is only one of them. Attention should be paid to clauses such as seller's warranty and the financing and inspection conditions.

The agreement of purchase and sale is a legal document that can cost you thousands of dollars and tremendous headaches if you do not pay close attention. Many people focus on the price but overlook other clauses in the agreement, hence creating problems on or before closing.

A professional real estate agent will tell you all the facts and will try her/his best to make you aware of your obligations, hence lowering your risks.

A Professional Real Estate Agent

Not all real estate agents are competent and professional, so you should spend time in selecting your agent. Some sellers will interview a few agents before they sign a listing agreement with one of them. A professional real estate agent should:

i. Have professional knowledge

> The agreement of purchase and sale in a real estate transaction is often drafted by your agent. Although there are preprinted forms for them to use, all other clauses are worded by your agent (or to be inserted by her/him). S/he should be able to explain those legal clauses in plain language to you. Each clause s/her uses should be well constructed and protects you without destroying the fairness of the deal.

ii. Have professional ethics

> Real estate agents are not supposed to push their clients to accept any offer, then close the deal, get the commission and say goodbye. Being real estate sales practitioners, they are the agents for the buyers when there is a buyer agency agreement between them. Agents, like lawyers and accountants, are responsible to their principal and owe their client various fiduciary

duties. In real estate, one of the duties of a buyer's agent is to buy you the property you want at as low a price as possible.

iii. Have professional selling skills

Some think an aggressive salesperson is a successful agent, but more believe a successful agent need not be aggressive. A professional agent will not push her/his clients to make decisions as s/he respects their judgment. They rely on long-term relationships, not a one-time deal. Therefore, they are tough negotiators with the other parties but friendly consultants with their clients.

Buyer's Agency

Some people like to buy the property themselves without employing their own real estate agent. Since most of the properties in the market for sale are listed with real estate brokerage firms, these people will either need to deal with another agent directly without their own agents or work with the listing agent, thus creating a dual agency relationship.

The weakness of dual agency

When a real estate agent represents both the seller and buyer, s/he is called a dual agent. The practice of a dual agency relationship should be discouraged, as it brings no benefit to either the seller or buyer. No one would retain the lawyer of the other party as one's legal counsel when one goes to court. The same logic applies to real estate agents.

Under a dual agency situation, both the seller and buyer will receive service with limited representation. That is, the agent will still assist both the buyer and the seller, but s/he will not work to represent one party to the detriment of the other party. As a result, the seller should not expect her/his agent to negotiate the highest sale price for her/him and, the buyer cannot expect her/his agent will negotiate a good bargain for her/him. As a result, the agent brings no benefit to either the seller or buyer.

Whether you are buying or selling, I cannot see any reason for you to allow your agent to work for the other party as a dual agent. In such cases, your protections and rights will be lowered significantly.

Since a dual agent has the incentive of earning double commissions from one transaction, s/he may have the tendency to push her/his client(s) in order to make a deal. Therefore, a dual agency should always be discouraged and avoided.

Exclusive Buyer's Agent

More and more people resist the dual agency relationship since they know it brings no benefit to them. Accordingly, some real estate brokerage firms offer the exclusive buyer's agency service.

A brokerage that offers an exclusive buyer's agency will not take listings from the sellers, and therefore it will not be possible to create a dual agency. As a buyer's agent, it will try to negotiate the lowest price and most favourable terms for the buyers. It will point out the flaws of the property you are interested in so that you can make your decision objectively. It is obligated to disclose all the information it has about the seller and the seller's property that may benefit the buyer. Furthermore, it will perform a comparative market analysis to show you all the available properties that fall into your criteria. Last, it will provide opinions on the value of the property you like so that you can make your offer at a reasonable price.

The concept of buyer's agent has spread over the nation. More and more buyers are willing to sign a buyer's agency agreement with the real estate agents they work with, whether it is an exclusive buyer's agency firm or not.

12. Employing a Property Manager

If you have an investment property, you will have to spend extra time managing it. You have to maintain it, rent it out, communicate with the tenant, and pay all the expenses related to the property.

Property Management

Many people think real estate brokerage should include property management, but this is not the case. However, some landlords and tenants call their real estate agents regarding matters of their rented properties a few years after commencement of their lease. Fairly speaking, once a property is rented and the tenant has moved in, the real estate agent has done her/his job, and the landlord and tenant should communicate directly between themselves. If you need someone to look after your rental property (such as for out-of-town properties), employing a property manager is a good solution.

The Role of a Property Manager

Simply speaking, the duties of a property manager fall into four areas:

i. Keeping the property rented

ii. Collecting the property income

iii. Paying the property expenses

iv. Maintaining the physical integrity of the property

Although there are many similarities in managing residential properties and commercial properties, it is much more complicated in managing commercial properties such as shopping centers and office buildings. Since this book is written mainly for buyers of residential properties, we will concentrate on their management.

i. Keeping the property rented

> All landlords want their property to be fully rented and to generate the highest income. The first responsibility of a property manager is to keep the property rented. This duty does not include the role of a real estate agent when the property is rented through a real estate firm. If the landlord decides to employ a real estate agent to market the property, the burden of leasing is taken over by the agent from the property manager. Of course, the commission for the agent is to be paid by the landlord in addition to management fees.

ii. Collecting the property income

> Property income includes all rents of the premises, appliances and parking spaces and reimbursement from the tenants. When a tenant is delinquent, it is also the duty of the property manager to act on behalf of the landlord to evict the tenant and re-rent the property as quickly as possible to mitigate the loss.

iii. Paying the property expenses

> The landlord's costs can be reduced by using efficient and effective property management. Costs generally not covered in management fees include real estate commissions, repair and alternations, appraisals, additional accounting, special reports, tax appeal services

and all other consultation services.

iv. Maintaining the physical integrity of the property

A well-kept property can maximize earning potential for the landlord. It is the property manager's duty to maintain the premises in good condition. As noted above, the cost to repair is not included in management fees.

The Benefits of Employing a Property Manager

i. Time-Saving

Managing a property can be time-consuming even if the tenants are cooperative. Landlords will find that most of the time used in managing a property is in repairing the electrical appliances, maintaining the property, depositing tenant's checks and paying all the related expenses. Employing a property manager can save you all this time.

ii. Trouble free

If you have experienced evicting a tenant, you will know how distressing it is. When there are things in the property to be fixed, it costs you time as well. There was a case involving a tenant whose oven broke down once a month. His landlord did not want to continue 'taking care of' him, so she sold the property at a price lower than the market value in order to get rid of it fast.

iii. Efficiency and higher productivity

A property manager has the obligation to obtain the highest possible rents commensurate with the selection of top quality tenants for her/his landlord. Since property managers know the rental market well, they will set rents at a competitive rate to minimize vacancy losses and generate the highest productivity for their landlords.

Some real estate agents will also act as property managers for their clients. Many charge one-month rental as the management fee and the properties they manage are mostly houses and condo units. Some companies are not real estate brokerage firms but deal only with property management. They target mainly high-rise rental apartments and commercial properties. Their management fees range from 3 percent to 6 percent of the net operating income of the property.

It is a good idea to be your own property manager if you have time to deal with all the issues arising from the property and the tenants. This gives you direct contact with your tenants and allows you to know first hand of problems before they worsen. Saving your property management fee is not a major concern, although it is good to have the savings. This is particularly true when you have quite a few rental properties to look after. Some landlords quit their jobs and act as full-time property manager for their own properties.

13. Actions to Be Taken

"Discussed but not decided! Decided but not acted! Acted but not succeeded!" These are the statements I have used to describe some real estate investors.

Discussed but Not Decided!

Mr. Smith had more than $300,000 in his bank account and was looking for an opportunity to invest. He called two consultants to discuss his plan. One was a stockbroker, and I was the other one for real estate investment. I spent nearly three hours analyzing his investment goal, the risk he could bear and the type of properties that interested him.

I suggested that he divide his fund into three parts, one third to be invested in the stock market, one-third to be used to buy real estate, and the remaining one third to be left in the bank to produce cash income. This was exactly the suggestion by the other investment consultant. However, Mr. Smith said he had another plan, and it was to buy a franchise restaurant that would cost him more than $300,000. Therefore there was no decision on that day.

Two years later, Mr. Smith was still holding his $300,000 in his bank, with the interest rate at 1.5 percent. He did not buy anything, the stock market was up, the real estate market was up and the waiting time for that restaurant had two more years to go.

Decided but Not Acted!

Miss Jones was also interested in both the stock and real estate markets. She decided to buy $100,000 in stock and to invest another $100,000 in real estate. I recommended three two-bedroom condo units to her, and she was extremely interested in the one selling at around $150,000. However, she took no action when I followed up.

After several months, the real estate market grew and the prices of such units had gone up by several thousand dollars. Miss Jones was not willing to pay several thousand more for a unit similar to one she saw before. The result was that four years later such units sold for more than $200,000, and Miss Jones still had not bought any property.

Acted but Not Succeeded!

Mr. Lopes was a new immigrant, living in Tallahassee, Florida. Although his English proficiency was not high, he showed extreme interest in real estate investment. He once called me, enquiring about a 'rooming house', as he felt this type of property could give him an attractive return on investment. A rooming house is dormitory-style housing in existing single-family residential neighbourhoods. It is usually renovated from a house by altering its living room and dining room into separated bedrooms and renting out all the bedrooms in both upper and ground levels (usually more than five) to individuals. Rooming houses are usually found in an old downtown neighbourhood. My suggestion to him was that this kind of property certainly did not suit him because managing this kind of property needed good communication in English, as disputes among tenant would always occur, and rooming houses were not (at that time) regulated and might create problems. One example: not enough parking spaces for each tenant, an issue that might cause disputes.

In addition, the selling price of this kind of property is decided by the income generated by it (the net rent collectible), so the price would be much higher compared to the same size of ordinary houses. Instead of the attractions Mr. Lopes mentioned, the maintenance work at the property also caused my concern. However, Mr. Lopes, acting on his own, bought a rooming house at approximately $400,000.

A few months after he bought the rooming house, Mr. Lopes called me to seek advice again. One of his tenants owed him two months rent, and there was a quarrel among three other tenants over the use of the kitchen. He did not know how to handle them. The worst issue was that after reviewing the balance sheet of that fiscal year he learned that he was losing money on that property. Since the lender treated the rooming house as commercial property, accordingly the mortgage rate was higher than those for residential mortgages. Moreover, he was too optimistic about increasing the rent by a high percentage, as rents were well below the market rent. Unfortunately, he was unable to increase the rents when all the tenants raised their objections. He eventually lost more than $40,000 by selling it at the same price after two years.

If Mr. Lopes could have listened and relied on a professional real estate agent to act for him, he might not have lost money. In most cases, real estate buyers do not have to pay any commission to their agents (not out-of-pocket). Therefore, I cannot see any reason for not using a professional agent to protect your interest when you are buying.

Act Now

You have to have a plan for your real estate investment (remember buying a home is also an investment) in order to make it a successful one. The steps are: Discuss, Decide, Act and Succeed. First, you should discuss with your family members and your agent to find out the most suitable property to buy;

ask your banks or mortgage broker for the best mortgage available, and consult with your accountant or counsel for tax advice. Second, you should make your decision objectively based on your own situation and requirements. Once you have decided what type of property to buy, you should actively look for it. Buying a property is not a difficult task, but you have to commit yourself to it.

So act now, go out to find a suitable property for yourself or start saving your down payment. Just remember the name of this book: Real Estate; Everyone Can Afford It!

Appendix A
Annual Property Operating Data Form

Name _____   Date _____
Location _____   Price $ _____
Type of Property _____   Debt $ _____
Size of Property _____ Sq. Ft. Units   Equity $ _____

Mortgage	Amount	Payment	Interest	Term/Amt
1st	_____	_____	_____	_____
2nd	_____	_____	_____	_____
3rd	_____	_____	_____	_____

ALL FIGURES ANNUAL $/Sq. Ft. or $/Unit %   COMMENTS / FOOTNOTES

POTENTIAL RENTAL INCOME _____ _____

   - Vacancy & Credit Losses _____ (_____ % of $ _____)

= EFFECTIVE RENTAL INCOME _____ _____

   + Other Income _____ _____

= GROSS OPERATING INCOME _____ _____

OPERATING EXPENSES:

Real Estate Taxes _____ _____

+ Property Insurance _____ _____

+ Off-Site Management _____ _____

+ Payroll On-site Personnel _____ _____

+ Expenses / Benefits _____ _____

+ Taxes _____ _____

+ Repair and Maintenance _____ _____

+ Utilities

  Water _____ _____

  Electricity _____ _____

  Gas/Oil _____ _____

  Others _____ _____

\+ Accounting and Legal _____ _____

\+ Real Estate Leasing Commission _____ _____

\+ Advertising / Licenses / Permits _____ _____

\+ Supplies _____ _____

   + Miscellaneous _____ _____

= TOTAL OPERATING EXPENSES

GROSS OPERATING INCOME − TOTAL OPERATING EXPENSES

   = NET OPERATING INCOME _____ _____

   − Annual Debt Service _____ _____

= CASH FLOW BEFORE TAXES

Appendix B
Cash Flow Analysis Form

Property Name: _____

Down Payment: _____

+ Costs of Acquisition: _____

= Investment at Purchase: _____

+ Debt: _____

= Acquisition Price _____

Mortgage Data

Mortgage Data	Beginning Balance	Term / Amortization	No. of payments per year	Interest Rate	Payment	Annual Debt Service	Remarks
1st Mortgage							
2nd Mortgage							
3rd Mortgage							

Taxable Income

	Year 1	Year 2	Year 3	Year 4	Year 5
Potential Rental Income					
Minus: Vacancy & Credit Losses					
Equals: Effective Rental Income					
Plus: Other Income					
Equals: Gross Operating Income					
Minus: Operating Expenses					
Equals: **Net Operating Income**					
Minus: Non Operating Expense					
Minus: Interest – 1st Mortgage					
Minus: Interest – 2nd Mortgage					
Minus: Interest – 3rd Mortgage					
Minus: Amortization of Loan Fees					
Equals: Subtotal Taxable Income Before CCA					
Minus: Allowable CCA					
Equals: Real Estate Taxable Income					
Times: Marginal Tax Rate					
Equals: **Tax Liability**					

Cash Flows

	Year 1	Year 2	Year 3	Year 4	Year 5
Net Operating Income					
Minus: Annual Debt Service (1st)					
(2nd)					
(3rd)					
Equals: Cash Flow Before Taxes					
Minus: **Tax Liability**					
= Cash Flows After Tax					

Appendix C
Sales Proceeds Work Sheet

Property Name:_____

Mortgage Balances	Year 1	Year 2	Year 3
Principal Balance - 1st Mortgage			
Principal Balance - 2nd Mortgage			
Principal Balance – 3rd Mortgage			
TOTAL UNPAID PRINCIPAL			

PROJECTED SALES PRICES (after commission)			

RECAPTURED CAPITAL COST ALLOWANCE (RCCA)

Acquisition Price			
Minus: Total Soft Costs			
Minus: Original Land Allocation			
Equals: Improvement Allocation at Purchase (A)			
Plus: Capital Improvements			
Minus: CCA Taken			
Equals: UCC Improvement at Sale (B)			
Improvement Allocation on Sale (C)			
Lesser of (A) and (C)			
Minus: (B)			
Equals: **RCCA**			

ADJUSTED COST BASE

Acquisition Price			
Minus: Soft Costs Allocated			
Plus: Capitalized Items			
Plus: Unamortized Soft Costs			
Minus: Partial Sales			
Equals: **Adjusted Cost Base**			

GAIN OR CAPITAL GAIN

PROJECTED SALE PRICE			
Minus: **Adjusted Cost Base**			
Minus: Costs of Sale			
Equals: Gain or Capital Gain			
Minus: Capital Gain Exemption			
Equals: Capital Gain			
Taxable Capital Gain (% of Capital Gain)			

TAX LIABILITY ON SALE

RCCA			
Plus: Gain OR Taxable Capital Gain			
Minus: Unamortized Expenses			
Equals: Taxable Income on Sale			
Times: Marginal Tax Rate			
Equals: **Tax liability on Sale**			

SALE PROCEEDS

PROJECTED SALE PRICE			
Minus: **Adjusted Cost Base**			
Minus: Mortgage Balance(s) (from top of form)			
Equals: Proceeds Before Taxes			
Minus: **Tax liability on Sale**			
Equals: **SALE PROCEEDS AFTER TAX**			

Appendix D
(Sample Agreement, to be used with an Agreement of Purchase and Sale)
OPTION TO BUY

THIS AGREEMENT made this _____ day of _____, 20_____.

BETWEEN: _____
(hereinafter called the 'Optionee') OF THE FIRST PART

AND: _____
(hereinafter called the 'Optionor') OF THE SECOND PART

1. In consideration of the sum of _____ US Dollars ($_____.00) paid by the Optionee to the Optionor, the receipt of which is hereby acknowledged, and in consideration of the Lands hereinafter recited, the Optionor grants to the Optionee the sole and exclusive option irrevocable within the time provided for exercise herein, to buy the Lands referred to in the Agreement of Purchase and Sale attached hereto and initialed by the parties for identification.

2. The Option hereby granted shall be open for acceptance by the Optionee on or before, but not after, the _____ day of _____, 20_____, and may be exercised by the Optionee giving written notice of exercise of Option, delivered to the Optionor at his usual place of business, failing which this Option shall become null and void and the Optionor shall be entitled to retain the consideration paid for granting the Option.

3. Exercise of this Option shall constitute an Agreement of Purchase and Sale between the Optionor and the Optionee at the price, and upon the terms, set forth in the said Agreement of Purchase and Sale, as if the said Agreement of Purchase and Sale was made by the Optionee and accepted by the Optionor on the date this Option was exercise.

4. It is agreed and understood that the Optionee and his agent can advertise to sell the land, including but not limited to erect a For Sale sign on the said land, and the Optionee can assign this Option without the Optionor's consent within the time provided for exercise herein, and there is a potential of significant gain in price when the Optionee sell this option to a third party.

5. The Closing date of the Agreement of Purchase and Sale shall be thirty (30) days after the date Optionee exercises this Option. In the event that this scheduled closing day is not a business day for the relevant Land Registry Office, the closing shall then be the next immediate day that the relevant Land Registry Office is open for business. Requisition date shall be Fourteen (14) days before the closing date.

6. Time shall be in all respects the essence hereof.

7. This Agreement shall be read with such changes of gender or number as may be required by the context.

8. The heirs, executors, administrators, successors and assigns of the undersigned are bound by all the terms herein.

Dated at _____ this _____ day of
_____ year _____.

SIGNED, SEALED   IN WITNESS whereof I have hereunto set my hand
AND DELIVERED   and seal:
in the presence of:

_____   _____   ✸   _____
(Witness)   (Optionee)   (Seal)   (Date)

The Undersigned grants the above Option.

Dated at _____ this _____ day of
_____ year _____.

SIGNED, SEALED   IN WITNESS whereof I have hereunto set my hand
AND DELIVERED   and seal:
in the presence of:

_____   _____   ✸   _____
(Witness)   (Optionor)   (Seal)   (Date)

Appendix E
Sample Agreement of Purchase and Sale

THIS AGREEMENT made this _____ day of _____, 20_____.

BETWEEN: _____
(Hereinafter called the 'Buyer') OF THE FIRST PART

AND: _____
(Hereinafter called the 'Seller') OF THE SECOND PART

1. THE REAL PROPERTY

Buyer agrees to buyer from the Seller the real property located at _____ in the City of _____ and having a frontage of _____ feet (more or less) by a depth of _____ feet (more or less) and legally described as _____
_____.

2. CONSIDERATION AND FINANCING

The purchase price for the real property shall be the sum of _____
_____US Dollars
($_____.00), payable as follows:

    a)   Buyer agrees to submit a sum of _____ Dollars ($_____.00) by cheque to the Seller's lawyer in trust immediately after all conditions in this Agreement have been waived, as a deposit to be held by it pending completion or other terminating of this Agreement and to be credited on account of the purchase price on Closing.

    b)   THIS OFFER IS CONDITIONAL upon the Buyer

arranging, at his own expense, a new First Mortgage that is satisfactory to him. Unless the Buyer gives notice in writing delivered to the Seller by 11:59 p.m. on the 5th business day after the acceptance of this offer, that this condition is fulfilled, this Offer shall be null and void and the deposit shall be returned to the Buyer in full without interest. This condition is included for the sole benefit of the Buyer and may be waived at his option by notice in writing to the Seller within the time period stated herein.

c) The balance of the Purchase Price, subject to the adjustments to a transaction of this nature and those provided for herein, shall be paid on Closing to the Seller by certified check or by bank draft.

3. IRREVOCABILITY

This Offer shall be irrevocable by the Buyer until the _____ day of _____, 20____, at 5:00 p.m. Eastern Time, after which time, if not accepted, this Offer shall be null and void and the deposit shall be returned to the Buyer in full without interest.

4. COMPLETION DATE

This Agreement shall be completed by no later than 5:00 pm on the _____ day of _____, 20___. Upon completion, vacant possession of the property shall be given to the Buyer unless otherwise stated in this Agreement.

5. TITLE

The Buyer is to be allowed until 5:00 pm on the ____ day of _____, 20 ____ to examine title at his expense. If, within that time, any valid objection to title is made in writing to the Seller, or its present use _____ may not be lawfully continued or the principal building may not be insured against risk of fire, which the Seller shall be unable to remedy and which the Buyer will not waive, then, notwithstanding any intermediate acts or negotiations in respect of such objections, this Agreement shall be null and void and the deposit shall be returned to the Buyer in full forthwith with interest accrued thereon.

6. NOTICES

Any notice, direction or other communication required or permitted to be given to the Buyer or to the Seller hereunder, shall be in writing and may be given by having the same delivered by hand or sent by means of printed electronic or printed telephonic communication or sent by prepaid registered or certified mail addressed to the Buyer or Seller, as the case may be, as follows:

(a)   To the Buyer:

Address: _____

_____

_____

Fax number: _____

(b)   To the Seller:

Address: _____

_____

_____

Fax number: _____

Unless otherwise provided for herein, any such notice, direction or other communications as aforesaid, delivered, or transmitted shall be deemed to have been delivered on the date on which it was delivered or transmitted or if mailed, then seventy-two (72) hours following the date of mailing, and any time period referred to in a notice commences to run from the time of delivery or transmission or seventy-two (72) hours following the date of mailing. If there is a reasonable possibility that the postal service may be interrupted or substantially delayed due to actual or anticipated labor disputes, any notice, direction or other communications shall only be delivered in person or transmitted as aforesaid. Either party may at any time give notice in writing to the other, of any change of address of such party for the purpose of giving any notice herein. Any notice electronically transmitted to the recipient on a non-business day or after business hours shall be deemed to have been received during business hours on the next business day.

7. REPRESENTATION BY SELLER

The Seller represents and warrants which representations are being relied upon by the Buyer and which representations shall be conditions for the closing and which shall be conditions precedent to the obligations of the Buyer to complete the Purchase of the Property at the closing, but any one or more of which may be waived unilaterally by the Buyer at its election by notice in writing to the Seller or the Seller's lawyer at or before the closing date that:

a) The Seller covenants with the Buyer and warrants that it is the beneficial owner of the Property with good and marketable title thereto and has full right and authority to convey the Property to the Buyer.

b) The Seller covenants with the Buyer and warrants that the said building and appurtenances are situated wholly within the limits of the lands to be conveyed and comply with all zoning by-laws and setbacks, and no building, fences or other structures on adjoining lands encroach on or over the said lands. To satisfy this warranty, the Seller hereby agrees to provide at her/his expense to the Buyer within 3 days following acceptance of this offer, with a copy of an existing survey. If there is no survey available from the Seller or the survey provided is not acceptable to the Buyer's lawyer or lender, then the Seller hereby agrees to pay the cost of placing a policy of title insurance on the subject property on or before the closing date.

c) The Seller covenants with the Buyer and warrants that the buildings and structures erected on the subject lands, furniture, equipment and facilities (including parking facilities) provided therein and thereon, and the use thereof, conform to all requirements of Federal Government, State Government, City and other laws, regulations and by-laws, including all zoning restricted area by-laws of the County or City where the buildings are situated and the buildings and equipment thereon are in a state of good condition and good repair.

d) The Seller covenants with the Buyer and warrants that, there are no outstanding work orders by any Local or State Government authorities with respect to the buildings and appurtenances and that there are no outstanding requirements or active file with such government authorities requiring work to be done to the subject land and premises.

e) The Seller agrees to provide to the Buyer's lawyers within three (3) days of receipt letters of authorization to the building, health, fire, electricity, zoning and environmental and hazard and waste departments permitting the said Departments to conduct an inspection of the said premises and to release any information with respect to such inspections to the Buyer's lawyers. Such letters of authorization shall be prepared by the Buyer's lawyers and furnished to the Seller's lawyers for review prior to the Seller's execution.

f) The Seller covenants with the Buyer and warrants that the Seller has not entered into any contract for the servicing, maintenance or management of the lands, buildings fixtures, and equipment subject to the herein transaction which may be binding upon the Buyer or affect the subject property other than those disclosed in this Agreement or delivered to Buyer as provided herein.

g) The Seller covenants with the Buyer and warrants that the property is not subject to expropriated proceedings by the Local or State Governments and that the Seller has no knowledge of any intention on the part of such government bodies to expropriate the property being sold herein.

h) The Seller shall on or before closing at its own expense obtain and register discharges of all liens, mortgages or encumbrances, save and except any city development or site plan agreements.

8. RIGHT TO ASSIGN

It is understood and agreed between the Parties that the Buyer shall have the right at any time prior to closing, to assign this Agreement to an individual, persons, a partnership or a company, either existing or to be incorporated, without consent of the Seller. Upon delivery to the Seller of notice of such assignment, together with the assignee's covenant in favor of the Seller to be bound hereby as Buyer, the Buyer hereinbefore named shall stand released from all further liability hereunder.

9. CHATTELS INCLUDED

The following chattels are included in the purchase price and will stay with the property after closing:

_____

_____

_____

_____

10. FIXTURES EXCLUDED

The following fixtures are not included in the purchase price and will be removed before closing:

_____

_____

11. RENTAL ITEMS

The following items are rented and are not included in the purchase price. The Buyer agrees to assume the rental contracts if they are assumable:

_____

_____

12. INSPECTION

Buyer acknowledges having inspected the property by himself or a certified inspector prior to submitting this Offer and understands that upon Seller accepting this Offer there shall be a binding Agreement of Purchase and Sale between Buyer and Seller.

13. RISK AND INSURANCE

Until completion of sale, all buildings, fixtures and equipment on the property shall be and remain at the risk of the Seller until closing and the Seller will hold all policies of insurance affected on the property and the proceeds thereof in trust for the parties hereto, as their interests may appear. In the event of damage to the said buildings, fixtures, equipment and chattels, before the completion of this transaction, the Buyer shall have the right to take such proceeds and complete the purchase or cancel this Agreement, whereupon the Buyer shall be entitled to the return of his deposit moneys in full forthwith together with accrued interest thereon.

14. TIME LIMITS

Time shall be in all respects the essence hereof

15. ADJUSTMENTS ON CLOSING

Unearned rentals, taxes, local improvements, water and assessment rates and fuel to be apportioned and allowed to the actual closing date; revenue and expenses for the day of closing shall be assumed by the Buyer. The Buyer shall not be called upon to assume any bad debts or rental in arrears which shall be the Seller's responsibility to collect and the adjustments shall be prepared on the basis that all rental payable has been paid. There shall be no adjustments at closing in favor of the Seller for any capital accounts yet to be recaptured from the tenants.

16. AGREEMENT ON WRITING

If there is any conflict or discrepancy between any provisions added to this Agreement (include any Schedule attached hereto) and any provision in this printed portion hereof, the added provision shall supersede the printed provision to the extent of such conflict or discrepancy. There is no representation, warranty, collateral agreement or condition that affects this Agreement other than as expressed herein. This Agreement shall be read with all changes of gender or number required by the context.

Dated at _____ this _____ day of _____, 20_____.

SIGNED, SEALED IN WITNESS whereof I have hereunto set my hand
AND DELIVERED and seal:
in the presence of:

_____   _____   _____
(Witness)   (Buyer)   (Seal) (Date)

I, the undersigned Seller, agree to the above Offer.

Dated at _____ this _____ dayof _____, 20_____.

SIGNED, SEALED   IN WITNESS whereof I have hereunto set my hand
AND DELIVERED   and seal:
in the presence of:

_____   _____   ✱   _____
(Witness)   (Seller)   (Seal) (Date)

ACKNOWLEDGEMENT

I acknowledge receipt of my signed copy of this accepted Agreement of Purchase and Sale.

_____   _____
(Buyer)   (Date)

I acknowledge receipt of my signed copy of this accepted Agreement of Purchase and Sale.

_____   _____
(Seller)   (Date)

www.ingramcontent.com/pod-product-compliance
Lightning Source LLC
Chambersburg PA
CBHW030655220526
45463CB00005B/1790